The Mirror and the Veil

An Overview of American
Online Diaries and Blogs

AMSTERDAM MONOGRAPHS IN AMERICAN STUDIES

11

General Editor

Rob Kroes
Amerika Instituut
University of Amsterdam

The Mirror and the Veil

An Overview of American Online Diaries and Blogs

Viviane Serfaty

Amsterdam - New York, NY 2004

Cover illustration © 2004 by Marianne Eskenazi

An early version of parts of chapter one will appear in a forthcoming issue of the Journal of American Studies *(Cambridge University Press); parts of chapter three will appear in a collection of essays published by Editions Universitaires de Dijon; brief excerpts from chapter four and five were published in* Recherches Anglaises et Nord-Américaines (RANAM), *Université Marc Bloch, Strasbourg, in 2003 and 2004.*

The paper on which this book is printed meets the requirements of "ISO 9706:1994, Information and documentation - Paper for documents - Requirements for permanence".

ISBN: 90-420-1803-8
©Editions Rodopi B.V., Amsterdam - New York, NY 2004
Printed in the Netherlands

To Al, Aiyah, Charlie, Brian, Augustine,
Bev, Rachel, Carolyn, Debra, DeeGee,
Diane, Doug, Beth, Bitter Hag, Medea,
Erin , Terri, Bunt Sign, Jezebel,
Gingko, Greg, Jessamyn, Sam,
Rachel, Miriam, Vicki, Mary Anne,
Lisa, Columbine, Daze, Miles,
Kymm, Medea, Kevin, Natalie,
To all the other diarists, too numerous to
mention by name,
and most particularly to Shmuel,
for writing about themselves on the Internet
and giving me, and many others,
such fascinating texts to read, ponder, and
get impassioned about.

The Mirror and the Veil

An Overview of American Online Diaries and Blogs

Acknowledgements

I wish to acknowledge very gratefully the support given by Alain Cazade, whose enlightened advice and encouragements have been inspiring. Heartfelt thanks are due to Claude Lacassagne, whose comments have stimulated my thinking throughout the years, and while this work was in progress. I wish to extend my warmest thanks to Louise Thomson, whose careful reading of the finished manuscript has been invaluable. I am especially grateful to Marianne Eskenazi, who illustrated the cover and discussed with me many of the ideas developed in this book, spurring me on to rework some of them. I also wish to thank warmly my children and my friends. Without their abiding and wholehearted support, none of this would have been possible.

Miss Prism: I really don't see why you keep a diary at all.
Cecily: I keep a diary in order to enter the wonderful secrets of my life. If I didn't write them down, I should probably forget all about them.
[…]

Cecily: I am afraid you must be under some misconception. Ernest proposed to me exactly ten minutes ago. [*shows diary*]
Gwendolen: [*examines diary through her lorgnette carefully*] It is certainly very curious, for he asked me to be his wife yesterday afternoon at 5:30. If you would care to verify the incident, pray do so. [*produces diary of her own.*] I never travel without my diary. One should always have something sensational to read in the train.

Oscar Wilde, *The Importance of Being Earnest*, Everyman's Library, London, 1930, Act II, p. 367-383.

Introduction

The concept of online diaries and weblogs usually arouses mild disbelief among listeners, for whom the mere idea sounds oxymoronic. In social representations, diaries are first and foremost intimate writings and making them available online therefore appears to raise intractable privacy issues; diaries are believed to be basically private documents that should never get public exposure. As we shall see in the following study, literary critics as well as social scientists have largely put such notions to rest, but the whole undertaking seems to many to smack of exhibitionism, or even worse, to be plainly irrelevant. Still, and with utter disregard for the scepticism evinced by many, self-representational writing flourishes on the Internet under a variety of guises, creating or re-creating a wide array of forms of self-expression, and begging for explanations rather than bafflement, condescension and offhand dismissal. Describing these forms and discovering the functions of personal narratives online, will therefore be one of the major foci of the present study. The second aspect of this work has to do with the affinities between American civilization and diary writing, more particularly in the nineteenth century. However, one of my basic theoretical assumptions is that, for all their apparent and sometimes actual novelty, online diaries and weblogs are but the latest avatars in the long history of self-representational writing. The analysis of online diary – and weblog-writing will accordingly begin with a study of the historical development of the form.

1. Definitions

Literary historians tend to have widely divergent views as to the starting-point and the scope of the history of self-representational writing. For Georges Gusdorf, personal narratives start with the invention of writing. For him, "the very first man who set out to speak and write his name inaugurated a new mode of human presence in the world. Beginning with the very first one, any inscription is an inscription of the self, the signature of an individual who tacks himself onto Nature, thus affording himself room to reflect upon and to transmute its meaning" (Gusdorf 1991a: 22).[1] In another poetic expression of the same idea, Gusdorf writes that the invention of writing marks the passage from pre-history to history. "Writing enables direct access to the consciousness of individuals; we can hope to see the world through their eyes as reflected in their writing. 'A mirror in ink' in Michel Beaujour's words [...] enabling a transfer from the *inside* to the *outside*" (Gusdorf 1991b: 12).[2]

Gusdorf bases his views on the monumental study published by Georg Misch in 1907,[3] whose initial four volumes started with Ancient Egypt, Greece and Rome and ended with medieval Europe. Younger disciples then carried on his life's work and studied the history of autobiography from the Renaissance and up to the Enlightenment (Gusdorf 1991a: 19). This tradition considers a large variety of texts to be variants of self-representational writing: "life stories, letters, assorted confessions" (Gusdorf 1991a: 20);[4] even 'to do' lists, appointment books, as well as account books and curricula vitae are all seen as inscriptions of the self, albeit described as "the lowest degree of self-representational writing, [...] peripheral to the person's private reality" (Gusdorf 1991a: 23).[5]

Gusdorf's 1948 doctoral dissertation, started while he was a prisoner of war and completed under the guidance of French philosopher Gaston Bachelard, marked the beginning of his lifelong

---

[1]   "Le premier homme qui *prend la parole* pour dire et écrire son nom inaugure une nouvelle modalité de la présence de l'homme dans le monde. Toute écriture à partir de la première, est écriture de soi, signature d'un individu qui s'ajoute à la nature, se donnant ainsi la possibilité d'en redoubler en esprit et d'en transfigurer les significations". Emphasis in the text. My translation; unless indicated otherwise, all subsequent translations will be mine.

[2]   "L'invention de l'écriture marque le passage de la préhistoire à l'histoire. [...] L'écriture permet un accès direct à la conscience des individus ; nous pouvons espérer voir le monde avec leurs yeux au miroir de l'écriture. 'Miroir d'encre', selon la formule de Michel Beaujour [...], l'écriture permet un transfert du *dedans* au *dehors*". Emphasis in the text.

[3]   Georg Misch. 1907; rpt. 1931. *Geschichte der Autobiographie*. Leipzig Berlin: Teubner. Quoted by Gusdorf 1991a: 19.

[4]   "récits de vie, lettres confidences variées".

[5]   "ces carnets [...] se maintiennent à la périphérie de l'actualité intime de la personne".

dedication to the study of personal narratives. This early work, combined with a subsequent 1956 article, was tucked away in an obscure volume written mostly in German to honor the memory of German scholar Franz Neubert (Gusdorf 1956: 106-123). Yet it set the stage for widespread interest in the study of self-representational writing in France, and spawned a long line of students and disciples in the English-speaking world as well.

Unsurprisingly, however, the literary criticism of the seventies and eighties began the deconstruction of the edifice patiently erected by the instigator of the new field of study, much to his displeasure and even rage. In his later work, Gusdorf literally seethes with anger against the new developments in the field, and the chief target of his contempt is Philippe Lejeune's vision of the history and of the nature of the genre. Indeed Lejeune tightens the definition of the genre on the one hand, and on the other hand ascribes to Jean-Jacques Rousseau the role of initiator of the modern form of self-representational writing.

To Gusdorf, this is a gross misinterpretation as well as an unacceptable restriction of the field to France only. He lists the various bibliographies itemizing the accumulation of diaries, confessions and journals in Germany, Britain and America (Gusdorf 1991a: 56-60). He also shows that the English tradition definitely influenced Rousseau's work, not only because he was acquainted with Bunyan's autobiography, *Grace Abounding to the Chief of Sinners* (1666), through his Dutch publisher, but also because in 1766, he had met Boswell, who had kept a diary since 1762 (Gusdorf 1991a: 76).[6] Gusdorf accordingly does not shy away from berating Lejeune for his alleged ignorance on numerous occasions. Deriding him for his inability to read German and more particularly Misch's works, Gusdorf points out that the latter's four-volume history, combined with the three-volume continuation written by his followers, still stops far short of what Lejeune sees as a watershed for modern self-representational writing, i.e. Jean-Jacques Rousseau's *Confessions*, published in 1782 and 1789.[7] To Gusdorf, this proves beyond any shadow of a doubt that Lejeune's periodization is irredeemably wrong.

---

[6] Boswell's *Journal* was long considered to be lost before being eventually discovered in the nineteenth century. It was then published in eighteen volumes from 1928 to 1934.

[7] See for instance Gusdorf 1991a: 30: "certains frères ignorantins", i.e. "some ignoramuses"; see also Gusdorf 1991a: 55: "Or cette œuvre savante, demeurée inachevée, s'arrête en fait avant le point origine considéré par Lejeune comme le commencement du commencement, le 'milieu du XVIIIè siècle'. Interrogé sur ce point au moins bizarre, notre auteur répond qu'il ne lit pas l'allemand, comme si cela

This Homeric and somewhat one-sided controversy – for Lejeune seems to have responded to these attacks with perfect restraint – has a bearing on the present study, inasmuch as online diaries may be said to represent but the latest avatar in the long history of self-inscription. To identify the historical roots of online diaristic writing and to try and discover its structural features, it is essential to position ourselves and take a stand on two distinct strands in this argument, the reason why diaries are written on the one hand, and the definition of diaristic writing on the other hand.

1.1. Religion, reason, desire

The ancestry of contemporary self-representational writing may be traced back to three major sources, each linked to a different tradition: Catholicism; English Puritanism; Libertines.[8] Plutarch's *Parallel Lives*, recounting the lives of great men, as well as the Roman practise of writing one's autobiography under the canonical title *De propria sua vita*, served as models for the religious and philosophical introspection carried out by St Augustine or St Theresa, who modified the pattern in their turn. The Catholic tradition may indeed be said to start with St Augustine's *Confessions* in the fifth century A.D., highlighting his spiritual journey and written for the edification of his contemporaries and of future generations. Other works using the first-person singular within Catholicism abound, two of the most famous such texts being St Theresa of Avila's *El Libro de Sua Vida*, and John Henry Newman's *Apologia Pro Vita Sua* in England, in the nineteenth century (Olney 1981: 28).

Seventeenth century England, shaken by political and religious upheavals, "forced people to search within themselves for compensations to the dismemberment of the outside world" (Gusdorf 1991a: 212).[9] Bunyan's autobiography, *Grace Abounding to the Chief of Sinners* (1666), may thus be said to constitute the second line of

---

l'autorisait à rejeter dans le néant tout ce qui a été écrit dans cet idiome", i. e.: "in fact, this learned, still unfinished work [i.e. Misch's], ends before the landmark considered by Lejeune to be the beginning of all beginnings, the middle of the 18th century. Asked about this bizarre quirk, to say the least, our author answers he cannot read German, as if that allowed him to cast into nothingness whatever was written in that language".

[8] For this insight on Libertines I am indebted to Jean Fabre's oral comments transcribed in Georges Gusdorf 1975: 998.

[9] "L'urgence des motivations politiques et religieuses superposées à ce surgissement de possibilités neuves oblige les hommes à chercher en eux-mêmes des compensations au démembrement du monde extérieur".

ancestry for self-representational writing. The Puritan journals were a requirement of religious self-discipline. Like the seventeenth century Quietist journals, they recounted a spiritual journey towards personal salvation. Self-representational writing plays an all-important part in this process, as an exercise in self-scrutiny and interpretation of everyday life events and experiences (Gusdorf 1991b: 445). In such texts, faith is exposed to the slings and arrows of the individual's experience of it, and the fear of being bereft of grace is permanent. The Puritan journal often is therefore an account of anxious and tortured journeys through the uncertainties of the soul (Gusdorf 1975: 988). But then again, the mere fact of becoming aware of one's fall from grace and of praying for its return amounts to an act of faith in the power of the self to rise from the slough of despond (Gusdorf 1991b: 445). Perhaps this is the reason why, from then on and well into the twentieth century, this inner sanctum became the supreme locus legitimizing all human actions and relations (Gueissaz 1995: 83), while at the same time seeking to contain within strict limits any disorderly emotions (Gueissaz 1995: 95).

In the seventeenth century, books of the self were also written by Libertines, whose philosophical views opposed the absolute power of kings and therefore incurred their wrath. This was paradoxically made possible by the very rise of absolutism itself which, by positing a law imposed on public behavior while remaining indifferent or neutral towards private behavior, instituted a separation between the private and the public self. Libertines thus displayed extreme freedom in their thinking and writings, while conforming strictly to the mores of their contemporaries in their public lives (Haroche 1995). The simultaneously scandalous and self-serving nature of such writings irritated contemporary critics. Interestingly, when Rousseau's *Confessions* were first published, Diderot disparagingly compared him to Cardano, whose *De Vita Propria* was widely read in the sixteenth and seventeenth century (Gusdorf 1975: 998).[10] While far from being a philosophical Libertine, since he lived in the sixteenth century, his autobiography caused much outrage because Cardano did not flinch from listing, with seeming candor, his character flaws, his eccentricities and quirks, and his sinful actions (Wolff 1991). Such unabashed forthrightness could easily pass for self-vindication and was accordingly as widely berated as the book was widely read.

---

[10] During the debate that followed Gusdorf's talk, Jean Fabre related Diderot's appraisal of Rousseau: "un impudent, un Cardan".

The first two strands briefly described here – Catholicism and
Puritanism – placed writings of the self under the aegis of religion.
Then the philosophical Libertines, followed by Enlightenment
philosophers, placed them under the aegis of Reason by developing
the concept of an inner space devoted to internal deliberation, thus
beginning the long secularization process of the form. Samuel Pepys'
diary, written between 1660 and 1669, is one of the landmarks of this
evolution. The institution of a private space, where thought could
roam freely, accelerated the paradigm shift that led the individual from
the situation of being under the sway of religion to the situation of an
individual fondly supposed to be ruled by reason in the seventeenth
and eighteenth century. Then a new paradigm shift occurred. Even
though his work undeniably stemmed from a long tradition, Jean-
Jacques Rousseau's posthumously published *Confessions* did indeed
mark the beginning of modernity inasmuch as the autobiographer
appeared to be ruled neither by religion nor by reason, but by desire.
The notion of the individual, already largely put in place by religious
thinking, was even further secularized and asserted its independence
from and opposition to society. The rise of desire as the prime mover
of humankind constituted the major change in self-conception
occurring in the middle of the eighteenth century and rippling down to
the present day, not least on the Internet.

1.2. Formal characteristics of self-representational writing

The second point requiring some elucidation is that of the
definition of self-representational writing and more specifically of the
diaristic form. To this end, I propose to use the definition given by
Lawrence Rosenwald in his masterful study of Emerson's diaries.
Based in part on Lejeune's conception of self-representational writing,
his views nevertheless differ on essential criteria. Rosenwald thus
writes:

> In form a diary is a chronologically ordered sequence of dated
> entries addressed to an unspecified audience. We call that
> form a diary when a writer uses it to fulfil certain functions.
> We might describe those functions collectively as the
> discontinuous recording of aspects of the writer's own life;
> more technically we might say that to call a text of the proper
> form a diary we must posit a number of identities: between the
> author and the narrator; between the narrator and the principal
> character; and between the depicted and the real, this latter
> including the identity between date of entry and date of
> composition. (Rosenwald 1988: 5)

Such a definition is particularly useful in that the criteria are both devoid of any reference to content and clearly defined, thus making it possible to exclude a number of affiliated but dissimilar forms: out go the 'to do' list, or the aspiring author's notebooks or the fictional autobiography. In addition, using the concept of "identity [...] between the depicted and the real" makes it possible to bypass the thorny issue of truth or, as Rosenwald puts it, of the fallacy of "veridicality" (Rosenwald 1988: 13).

This point is essential to the debate surrounding the very definition of diaristic writing. Lejeune indeed states that the autobiographical compact entered into by the writer guarantees that the latter is committed to telling the truth (Lejeune 1975: 13-46). In a similar vein, John Paul Eakin asserts that "autobiography is by definition a referential art [and] [...] the self that is its principal referent is in fundamental ways a construct of culture" (Eakin 1991: 15). On the other hand, Rosenwald, following Gusdorf's lead, argues that the self cannot be distinct from the very process of introspection (Rosenwald 1988: 14). For Gusdorf, "private life does not allow itself to be taken literally; it is not a prisoner to whatever discourse claims to depict it. [...] In such a perspective, self-representational writing is released from its promise of literal faithfulness to experienced reality" (Gusdorf 1991a: 13-14).[11] Put differently, this statement points at the fact that truth is constructed by diaristic writing, in an ongoing process of interpretation. Similarly, the question of "identity [...] between the author and narrator" must simply be interpreted so as to exclude any work of fiction, or any biography.

The issue of time is also accounted for by this description of diaries. Because there is little or no interval between the time of experience and the time of writing, personal diaries have both a fragmented approach to time and a continuous one. Fragmentation is due to the writing of each entry under a specific date, continuity is due to the regularity of the commitment to writing. None of these features, however, excludes editing or revising from the field of diaristic writing. Time may therefore intervene in a third way, as the hiatus between two or more versions of an entry.

Rosenwald's definition also excludes from its definitional field any autobiography, such as Benjamin Franklin's (1903) which, according to Pierre Pachet, is the first ever to have used self-representational

---

[11] "La vie personnelle ne se laisse pas prendre au mot ; elle n'est pas prisonnière du discours, quel qu'il soit, qui prétend la représenter. (...) Dans cette perspective, les écritures du moi se trouvent déliées du vœu de fidélité littérale à la réalité vécue".

writing as a path towards self-improvement (Pachet 2001: 11). Indeed, from their very inception, autobiographies encompass their own ending, because they mean to show the reader the author's progress from some point back in time to the time of writing itself (Lejeune 2000a: 213). This can also be found on the Internet, for instance in *Shmuel's Soapbox*, when the diarist includes two autobiographical essays written for the admissions committee of a graduate program.[12] In these texts, the diarist attempts to make sense of his whole life by making it fit into a pre-arranged pattern, so that all the events of his past life seem to converge towards this application for university admission. The enunciative pattern is thus comparable to a loop and is characterized by circularity and closure. Autobiographical self-representation also displays many of the features of self-justification and self-creation, displaying some kinship with judicial discourse, in which the autobiographer simultaneously plays the part of defendant, counsel and judge (Olney 1981: 22-23; Kuperty-Tsur 2000: 9). Hence autobiographies are essentially akin to apologia, and *The Confessions of St Augustine* can be said to have provided both a model and a foundation for them (Spengemann 1980: 32). The diary, by contrast, "must be conceived as a book of days and dates and intervals. Whatever functions a diary serves, the writer [...] chooses for them a form articulated by dates in chronological order, and a mode of writing spaced over time" (Rosenwald 1988: 6). Self-chronicling on the Internet may take either one of these two forms; our focus, however, will be the diaristic facet of self-representational writing with its patient, sometimes brilliant recording of the flotsam and jetsam of daily life and its back-and-forth movement between living and writing, which ends up irretrievably interweaving the life and the written word.

2. The ethics of Internet research

2.1. Accessibility of sources

In industrialized countries, the development of the Internet into a mass-medium over the past few years has predictably given increased visibility to previously underground or peripheral developments. Online conversations, once the province of computer scientists and students, are now part of the daily practises of large populations across all age ranges. In a similar fashion, online diaries have moved in the

---

[12]   *Shmuel's Soapbox* , Feb. 11, 2003 entry.
http://www.babeltower.org/soapbox/blog/2003_02_09_old.html.

span of a few years from an obscure geek-like activity to a phenomenon the mainstream press now writes about (Keller 1999; Rosenberg 1999; Wang 1999; Levy 2002).

The growth in Internet use has spurred the increasing interest of individual researchers, mostly in social sciences. The study of computer-mediated communication can be said to have turned into a fully-fledged field of research (Jones 1999), leading to a large number of attempts at conserving Internet material for future reference. National heritage institutions have accordingly begun archiving the contents of the Net. The large number of texts generated on message boards or in other venues is indeed not as ephemeral as was first thought by early Internet users and social commentators. Thus, messages posted to Usenet newsgroups have been archived since March 1997 by deja.com. When Google took over the company in 2001, the Usenet archive went offline but was promptly made available again after several activists protested. In addition, the cache system put in place by Google enables the consultation of pages for a certain amount of time even after they have been taken offline. Finally, the Wayback Machine[13], a public non-profit organization backed by the Library of Congress and the Smithsonian Institution, has been archiving snapshots of the Net at six-month intervals since the fall of 1996. Because it preserves sites with the entirety of their links, the Internet Archive gives greater permanence to Internet communication and contents and has enabled researchers to tap online material in the knowledge that their sources would remain accessible to others in the field.

2.2. Privacy

However, even though the impermanence of the Web may well turn out to be a fallacy, other contentious issues have yet to be dealt with in a definitive manner. One of them is that any research that takes the Internet as both means and medium has to address ethical issues regarding copyright and privacy. A research project about online diaries is doubly challenged by such issues, as its material is made up of sometimes very intimate outpourings written by easily traceable people. Even moderately knowledgeable Internet users can almost effortlessly find out a considerable amount of information about most diarists, up to and including their real names.[14] Many diaries reveal

---

[13] The Internet Archive, http://mail.archive.org/index.html
[14] This can be done with the help of a 'whois' search, for instance.

personal histories, or are used to work out painful issues, sometimes involving entire families.

Because they have had to deal with present-day questions and populations, social sciences have long evolved guidelines to help practitioners collect data while respecting individual privacy. This has not been the case for literary studies, inasmuch as they deal with fiction and as the very definition of fiction entails nearly complete freedom for both authors and critics. Privacy issues are irrelevant in a fictional world, although the diaristic genre, by introducing a concern for truth, may pave the way for veracity and referentiality issues being raised.

The present research, however, finds itself at the confluence of two disciplines: on the one hand, studying online diaries from a literary standpoint may shed light on the development of new forms of writing, and contribute to assessing the extent of this transformation and its meaning. On the other hand, viewing online diaries as primary sources may afford insight into the mores of ordinary people in contemporary America. In other words, studying online diaries may require approaches drawn from literary criticism as much as from social sciences – two disciplines with starkly different outlooks, methods and goals. Let us examine each one in turn.

2.3. Two approaches compared

A literary approach to online diaries rests on the assumption that, no matter how 'truthful' diarists purport themselves to be, their version of truth, of character, or of protagonist is a fictional construction (Anderson 2001: 17). As will become apparent, this theoretical hypothesis is a fertile one both offline and online. Ethically speaking, it means that personal writings on the Internet are not to be viewed as "slice-of-life" documents or faithful reflections of reality. Attention is instead focused on the internal logic of the text, seen as a self-contained, self-referential artifact.

By contrast, a social science approach to diaries entails taking into account the social dimension of this practise, and hence it entails securing the consent of the diarist through interaction of some kind, either email or more traditional forms of communication. According to the Association of Internet Researchers, observers "seeking informed consent need to make clear to their subjects how material about them and/or from them will be used – i.e., the specific uses of material and how their identities will be protected are part of what subjects are informed about and asked to consent to" (Ess 2002).

This requirement raises several problems. One of them is that obtaining the permission of a subject necessarily involves resorting to participant observation, a research methodology which is particularly appropriate to the fine-tuned understanding of human behavior, but which is also fraught with difficulties. Participant observation, which relies on direct contact with and immersion in a subject's activities, entails a number of specific distortions. Because observation modifies the observed, this approach obviously lays itself open to the charge of bias, precisely because it relies on direct interaction and hence empathy with the subject (Adler 1994: 377-392; Scharf 1999: 243-256). A way of systematizing observation and righting bias must therefore be devised.

When the subject of the research has to do with intimate writings, the difficulties of participant observation increase dramatically. Philippe Lejeune summarizes the problem thus: "Reading diaries, or interviewing diarists: in a perfect world, you could do both. The issue, however, is tricky. Reading the diary of a living person even as it is being kept, while simultaneously maintaining a relationship with the diarist, is closer to an intimate pact than to a scientific approach. No one ought to be encouraged to undertake such an adventure. Analyzing an interview is perilous enough as it is, even under a pseudonym. Dissecting a diary is even more hazardous" (Lejeune 1998: 174).[15] The 'intimate pact' Lejeune refers to – the exchange of correspondence almost imperceptibly leading to interpersonal relationships – is very likely to turn into an impediment, for at least two reasons. First, scrutinizing the diary of a person the researcher is acquainted with, and eventually publishing the results, might be assimilated to a breach of trust. In addition, familiarity is likely to induce reluctance to expose certain, sometimes unflattering, perhaps even sordid aspects of the diarist's life and thus might skew research towards a mild form of hagiography. I have therefore carefully eschewed any interaction with diarists when attempting to gain an insight into the phenomenon of online journaling as a whole.

---

[15] "Lire les journaux, ou interroger les diaristes: l'idéal serait bien sûr de combiner les deux. Mais la chose est délicate. Lire le journal, qui continue à être tenu, d'une personne vivante, avec laquelle on est en relation, c'est un pacte intime plus q'une démarche scientifique. On ne conseillera à personne de se lancer dans une telle aventure. Il est déjà périlleux, même sous un pseudonyme, d'analyser un entretien. Mais disséquer un journal…"

2.4. Anonymity

Another sensitive issue is that of anonymity. Concurring with Marvin (Marvin 1995), the Association of Internet Researchers recommends taking precautions and changing names or pseudonyms. Yet shielding identities may turn out to be materially impossible in an academic context, where footnotes are a requirement and the URLs of all the sites under observation have to be cited to enable verification.[16] Quoting from a diary therefore opens up the distinct possibility of its author being readily identified. This may not represent a difficulty for some diarists, who use their real names and sometimes even provide their addresses. Others, however, even while putting forth their writings on as public a medium as the Net, may strenuously object to academic scrutiny, not so much because of rather improbable possibilities of publicity, but for deeper, unconscious reasons, having to do with the very reasons why they undertook a diary. Bowing to the reluctance of such diarists would make the remaining ones a virtually self-selected sample, with the attendant distortions this would imply.

In addition, complying with the Association of Internet Researchers' recommendation to inform subjects of the uses to which the material will be put may represent daunting challenges, inasmuch as it ultimately amounts to granting them the right to oversee the research project. Many projects grow and develop through unexpected twists and turns and in unpredictable ways. This is indeed a defining feature of any research undertaking, and confining oneself to pre-determined orientations for the sake of privacy might end up hindering and perhaps sterilizing research.

2.5. Research hypothesis: the mirror and the veil

For all these reasons, my methodological choice in the present project has been different from the one recommended by the Association of Internet Researchers. I have assumed that the texts uploaded by diarists were certainly personal, often intimate but not private. Anyone who engages in self-representational writing on the Internet is not producing private material, but is engaging instead in "public acts deliberately intended for public consumption" (Paccagnella 1997). This implies diaries can be viewed as published literary works whose study demands compliance with copyright law and quotation rules, without, however, any further precautions regarding privacy or anonymity. My data gathering has therefore

---

[16]   Uniform Resource Locator, i.e. the address of an Internet site.

remained unobtrusive, while one of the questions I have tried to address is precisely the motivation of those, ever more numerous, who use the Internet to attempt a representation of the inner processes of the self. Assuming that the practitioners of self-representational writing are not necessarily the most reliable observers, I have attempted to work out an answer to that question without any reference to statements other than those included in the diaries themselves.

My research hypothesis rests on an interpretation of the complex apparatus of the computer. The technological set-up required for Internet access includes a computer screen, operating as a paradoxical, twofold metaphor, that of a veil and that of a mirror. The literal function of a screen is precisely to conceal and as a result of this perception, all kinds of highly controversial discourses are freely displayed on the Net. The screen seemingly offers a protection against the gaze of others, enabling each diary writer to disclose intimate thoughts and deeds, thus attempting to achieve transparency and breaking the taboo of opacity regulating social relationships. The screen, which mediates Internet access, thus establishes a dialectical relationship between disclosure and secrecy, between transparency and opacity (Serfaty 1999: 223). There is no such thing as private content on the Internet; the pretence of privacy is *de facto* shattered to pieces, since anyone can gain access to any site the world over, yet the diarists feel protected by the very size of the Internet.

How then can we account for the fact that the screen, which functions metaphorically as a veiling device, actually seems to enable diary writers to violate the codes of opacity instead of locking them into solipsism? The paradox lies in the invisibility seemingly enjoyed on the Internet by both writers and readers. Thanks to the screen, diarists feel they can write about their innermost feelings without fearing identification and humiliation, readers feel they can inconspicuously observe others and derive increased understanding and sometimes power from that knowledge. "Making oneself invisible means one no longer is a mere transparency anyone can see through, but that one has turned into a gaze that no taboo can stop" (Starobinski 1971: 302). The screen seems to allow diary-writers and readers both a symbolic re-appropriation of social space and the violation of social codes – a violation whose power derives from the persistence in real life of the taboo broken in a virtual space. Without the prohibition of intimate disclosure, there would be no transgression. The prohibition therefore is constitutive of the meaning of self-revelation on the Internet.

The screen can thus be said to function as a connecting space between the diary-writer and society. The computer screen is not only a device which keeps others at a distance but it is also a symbolic space where dreams and fantasies can be projected. These identity and personality fragments indeed spotlight some areas of the self, but the very action of bringing something to light renders other areas even more opaque, so that the screen is transformed into a mirror onto which diary-writers project the signifiers of their identity in an ongoing process of self-destruction and reconstruction.

The screen thus plays the part of the Other, of the ideal Other, because it is, in and of itself, empty and can thus be endowed with a plurality of meanings. It does not demand reciprocity, but only functions as a mirror of the self. And it is through such specularity that the private self can move beyond the limits imposed by social codes and connect with others in virtual space. The readers of online diaries all become mirrors for diary writers, reflecting and commenting on their every thought, and hence providing a social venue in which the private self can be deployed and reconnect with the social self.

Online diaries therefore pose a theoretical challenge because they can be seen as literary, personal and social spaces, and that for each of these aspects, specific methodological tools will have to be used. In fact, well-established analyses of diaristic narratives will be used to approach the new phenomenon and will perhaps contribute to pinpoint the defining features of the new medium whenever they fail to apply (Miller 1995). Thus, the examination of the literary and rhetorical features of online diaries will rest on a study of their underlying structures and on a comparison with traditional self-representational writing. Such a study will assess the links of this form with other, earlier texts and will use the tools of critical textual analysis to appraise the intertextuality of online diaries and of online self-representational practises.

Viewing diaries as personal spaces will entail studying the forms of the public-private divide and the meaning of the drive to publicize the intimate. Psycho-analytical tools will make it possible to investigate the significance of these evolutions. In addition, because online diaries often are long thought-out efforts to break with traditional representations of gender and self-identity, this study will approach the ways in which online diarists attempt to re-negotiate their relationship to their body-image and more generally to their identity.

Finally, assessing the social dimension of online diaries will lead us on the one hand to ascertain the affinities of Americans with this form, and on the other hand to describe and interpret the interactions between diarists and readers. Because diaries seem to have become a meaningful activity for so many readers, we shall discuss the notion of sociability brought into play by online diaries, relying on conceptual tools taken from social sciences. The combination of these three, sometimes divergent, approaches may indeed be necessary not only to grasp the specificities of Internet diaries, but also to outline their links with older forms of self-representational writing, thus exemplifying the need both to extend our methodological repertoire to take into account the complexity of online diaries, and to re-conceptualize cross-disciplinary approaches. Understanding a literary form cannot be done in full without an understanding of the symbolic and cultural stakes intertwined in even the seemingly most ethereal art form. The task of the literary researcher is indeed often extraordinarily close to that of the psychoanalyst or the social scientist, and nowhere is this truer than on the Internet, where forms of writing and multimedia communication overlap and cross boundaries, constantly and creatively hybridizing and in the process defying classification. But this very unruliness is the mark of the need for the researcher to attempt a full examination of the distinctiveness of online diaries through interdisciplinary approaches.

3. Corpus

The sample under examination in this analysis consists of forty-two personal diaries and blogs, all written by Americans, several of whom were born abroad -- Carolyn Burke in Canada, Mary Anne in Sri Lanka or Aiyah in Hong-Kong. The diarists being observed here are almost evenly divided between women and men and except for Mary Anne, who publishes erotica while finishing her dissertation, none of them is a writer by trade, although several are expressly using their diaries to hone their writing style. In addition to this sample, the present study also rests on the observation of twelve diarists' webrings containing literally thousands of diaries. Yet as my primary purpose in the present work is structure rather than content, I have chosen to narrow my focus and examine closely a limited number of instances. Structural approaches by definition transcend the individual while at the same time providing tools for the analysis of individual cases. The same methodological choice has led me to disregard the largely formal distinction between blogs and diaries to focus on the underlying features they share.

The sample was constituted randomly, through a search engine. The diaries and blogs that came under observation were then evaluated by two criteria; the first one was definitional, since any commercially oriented diary, often found whenever erotica is proposed, was kept out of the sample. Diaries and blogs primarily devoted to current events, politics or social commentary were also dismissed out of hand. Only diaries written by a single individual for non-professional purposes were included. The second criterion was content: entries had to consist of more than mere lists of annotated links to other websites. There had to be a clearly recognizable authorial voice responsible for each entry. As is apparent from these criteria, no claim for exhaustivity can be made, such a claim being precluded by the sheer infiniteness of Internet contents. I have instead chosen to focus on structure as a way to gain a purchase on the analysis of all diaries, through the in-depth examination of a few. The sample was studied from September 2001 through December 2003. In the course of such a long and regular interaction with these texts, some have acquired more presence and more character than others: the subjective element indeed cannot be removed from the researcher's stance and her own personality necessarily influences her choice of material. Some diaries have therefore been studied more closely than others, always keeping in mind, however, the characteristics common to all.

3.1. Value judgments

In view of the substantial growth in the number of online diaries and blogs, the question of value has to be addressed, if only so as to be dismissed. It is of course self-evident that from a specifically literary viewpoint not all diaries, whether online or offline, are of equal value; Gusdorf thus decries the trend toward the inclusion of obscure diarists in the realm of the study of self-representational writing (Gusdorf 1991a: 247). In stark contrast with this admonition, however, the present study rests on the assumption that the very existence of online diaries makes them worthy of study, in part because they extend and modify the traditional definition of the genre, as we shall see in the coming chapters, and in part because of the intrinsic worth of the material. The literary nature of such texts is not an issue in the present study, nor is the setting up of a canon along aesthetic criteria. What matters is that the private writings men and women offer to the attention of the world can provide an insight into the contemporary American ethos and give access to a form of writing in the making. The point in the present study therefore is to scrutinize a form that is rapidly gaining acceptance and is accordingly increasingly widespread. Even though online diaries and weblogs have already developed their own celebrities, and awards for writing excellence are given at regular intervals, the issue of literary value judgments remains irrelevant in this context, in the first place because a literary value scale is by definition hard to design, much less to apply. Fraught distinctions between high and low, elite and popular literature interfere with any attempt at appraisal. Secondly, although traditional literary criticism deals primarily in the literary canon, fierce challenges from recent scholarship have attempted to eradicate the very notion of a canon, and have been successful in replacing the vertical and exclusive hierarchies of yore with a more horizontal and inclusive pattern. The contemporary textual student therefore need not be concerned with issues of value judgments or hierarchies. In fact, it is necessary to forego completely the issue of value if one is to use a structural approach. Examining such forms regardless of the literary value they may possess or not is the only approach that gives empirical access to emerging literary models or evolving behaviors in America, both with regard to self-construction and the perception of the Internet.

3.2. The researcher's stance

Another of the specificities of this research is that the Internet is at the same time its subject and its tool. Not only is the raw material for this study gleaned directly from the network, but the network itself provides the tools necessary to approach this subject. In addition, the Internet is very much part and parcel of this particular researcher's life; the interweaving of the researcher and of her subject must be subjected to analysis, so as to detect the predictable distortions resulting from this situation. What might indeed be expected is excessive identification with the subject of the research, since I cannot envision myself to be exterior to the representations and the practises I am studying; I cannot view myself as being above, and detached from the subject of my research. This closeness may give rise to a series of impediments to analysis: "participation in the belief system inherent in the field, [...] disregard for the relevant information because it supposedly goes without saying, the illusion of immediate understanding and the related inability to question what appears to be above questioning" (Mauger 1999: 118).[17] In spite of these hurdles, researchers have to carve for themselves a position enabling them to grasp their research subject without being overwhelmed by it. It is therefore necessary to analyze the personal dimension which presides over the choice of a field of research and the development of working hypotheses.

As shown by Gaston Bachelard, there is no such thing as 'objective' observation (Bachelard 1970). Not only does the researcher always interfere with the subject under consideration, but this interference is required to develop the concepts necessary to the understanding of the subject. In other words, distortion is the very condition any research has to labour under. A sociologist, Alain Médam, pushes even further this vision of the intricate relationships between researchers and their fields, claiming that neutrality is out of reach, beset by involvement and bias (Médam 1983: 67).

However, becoming aware of the limits to one's neutrality does not mean that a subject cannot be accurately thought through. Such a realization does impose, however, a transversal approach to the research field as the most appropriate means to grasp its meaning with the least amount of bias. This is the reason why this work resolutely crosses over disciplinary boundaries: placed under the banner of multi-disciplinarity, at the crossroads between literary criticism and American studies, it is an attempt at ascertaining the structures of a phenomenon already characterized by its uncertain boundaries. A cross-disciplinary approach is a way of trying to make methodology coincide with a fundamentally polymorphous research subject, so as to attempt to grasp its meaning while preserving its inherent complexity.

---

[17] "La participation à la croyance inhérente au champ, [...] l'indifférence à l'information pertinente tant elle va de soi, l'illusion de la compréhension immédiate et l'incapacité corrélative de constituer comme faisant question ce qui paraît hors de question".

Chapter One

Offline and Online Diaries

1. Bits and Bytes

Online diaries are at once thoroughly familiar and intensely new. Their publication on the Internet may be seen to be upholding a long tradition in self-representational writing even as information technology modifies the forms and some of the functions of such texts.

Online diaries became widespread in or around 1995: as the number of households connected to the network increased throughout the United States, diaries were posted on individual homepages mostly by programmers or computer scientists. A few samples of these early attempts, beginning in January 1995, can still be seen on the Online Diary History Project.[1] Interestingly, of the thirty-two diaries listed as having started between 1995 and 1997, eighteen, or over fifty percent, are still active today. These early diaries mostly reproduced the stark simplicity of a notebook's layout, with black print on a white background. This simplicity was required by the HTML code itself,[2] which was the only tool available to publish any kind of content, whether scientific or personal. Gradually, however, and perhaps as a result of the development of greater aesthetic expectations, coupled with the rejection of the austere sobriety of the beginnings of the new medium, plain HTML coding was supplemented by the use of all the tools the Internet afforded, be it graphics, pictures, video or audio files. Still, online diaries could be posted only by those who had at least minimal skills in web design.

---

[1]   http://www.diaryhistoryproject.com. Accessed September 2001 and *seq.*
[2]   Hyper Text Mark Up Language, the publishing language of the World Wide Web.

1.1. From diary to weblog

Two further developments modified the situation: first, around 1997, Internet providers started offering free space for homepages. They gave the public several pre-set models making it possible to upload text and pictures. The personal web page was thus made accessible to the non-technologically minded and could become a space for one's daily musings.

The second major development was that of weblogs (Blood 2000). Weblogs started out as lists of annotated links to other sites, providing background, context or comment. According to Dave Winer, one of the earliest practitioners and creators of weblogging code (Winer 2002), the very first blog may be said to be that of Tim Berners Lee, the inventor of the World Wide Web, who posted his personal comments together with a few hypertextual links evaluating one year's achievements in online computing (Berners-Lee 1992). Thus, if we accept Winer's definition – a personal slant on any subject combined with hypertextual links to other sites – the weblog concept was initiated as early as 1992.

From the simple, pragmatically-oriented document still archived at the World Wide Web Consortium, weblogs progressively expanded to include the author's thoughts on a variety of topics as well as rants about current events. The real breakthrough, however, occurred around 1995 when several companies[3] offered a ready-made blank frame on which one could type whatever one wanted. The ready-to-use template was then uploaded by the company, which also offered to create a site for free if needed; the technological knowledge requirement was thus completely bypassed. All and sundry could now post their thoughts on the Internet without possessing any coding skills and with minimal Web literacy.

1.2. Terminology

As frequently happens, the new form gave rise to new words to refer to it. The idiom 'web log' was modelled on traditional ship's logs and the word 'log' itself had long been used to refer to the recording of chat sessions on instant messaging channels such as IRC

---

[3]   Blog-city, Blogspot.com, Blogger.com, Diaryland, LiveJournal, Pitas, TypePad, Weblogger and Xanga are considered to be leaders in the business. Source: "The Blogging Iceberg", *Perseus White Papers*, http://www.perseus.com/blogsurvey. Accessed October 2003.

or ICQ^4. However, as the popularity of weblogs grew, the term that had been coined to refer to the new kind of writing underwent a transformation. Some either mistakenly or humorously pronounced it [wi: -blog], thus coining the verb 'to blog' (Blood 2000). In a similar process of familiarization through abbreviation, 'webloggers' became known as 'bloggers'.

This abbreviation turned out to be linguistically productive, because the next, almost instantly popular coinage, was that of the word 'blogosphere', by a self-described computer geek, science fiction writer and blogger called William Quick, who formed a portmanteau word merging 'blog' and the Greek *logos* which, to him, was expressive of the way blogs operated (Quick 2001).[5] Lexical creativity did not end in 2001 and many new words have appeared, up to and including a weblog entitled "Blaugustine", in an apparently unwitting nod to the illustrious ancestor of self-representational writing.[6] Such developments, based as they are on folk etymology, have elicited the exasperation of some: "Blog. Blogorrhea. Blogosphere. Blogistan. Blogdex. Blogrolling. Warblogging.[7] Where will it all end ? [...] I wish someone had gotten to the naming committee before this whole movement got rolling. I hate the word 'blog,' but I like the format, particularly as a writer" (Alterman 2003: 85). This nearly schizophrenic attitude, and its back-and-forth movement between annoyance and enthusiasm, probably underlies

---

[4] Internet Relay Chat is an instant multi-channel communication system; ICQ is an approximate transcription of 'I seek you' and refers to an instant messaging system.

[5] " I PROPOSE A NAME [sic] for the intellectual cyberspace we bloggers occupy: the *Blogosphere*. Simple enough; the root word is *logos*, from the Greek meaning, variously: In pre-Socratic philosophy, the principle governing the cosmos, the source of this principle, or human reasoning about the cosmos; Among the Sophists, the topics of rational argument or the arguments themselves. (The American Heritage® Dictionary of the English Language)". Emphasis in the text.
http://www.iw3p.com/DailyPundit/2001_12_30_dailypundit_archive.php#8315120. Accessed February 2002.

[6] http://www.nataliedarbeloff.com/blaugustine.html

[7] Blogistan refers to a writer's weblog called Radio Free Blogistan. http://radiofreeblogistan.com. Blogdex.com is an MIT research project which evaluates the propagation of ideas in blogs by counting links; Blogrolling.com is a company that offers link management software; warblogging refers to the numerous diaries devoted to the war in Iraq, the most famous one being that of an Iraqi male nurse, Salam Pax, whose blog has been recently published: http://dear_raed.blogspot.com/. See S. Pax, "I became the profane pervert Arab blogger," *The Guardian*, Sept. 9, 2003. Accessed September 2003. http://www.guardian.co.uk/g2/story/0,3604,1038208,00.html.

much of the success of the form, be it among practitioners or readers, as it feeds on the ambivalence it elicits (Serfaty 2000: 238).

1.3. Modes of operation

Since 1997, when they began in earnest, blogs have evolved into a variety of genres. A large number of weblogs function as directories to other contents on the Net while also including news commentary, personal rants about current events, such as   Conservative Glenn Reynolds' *Instapundit*,[8] or thoughts about social issues and technology, like *Rebecca's Pocket* or *BoingBoing*.[9] Starting in 2002, a convention held at Harvard University has brought together practitioners of this sort of blogging and social scientists.[10] Alternatively, weblogs may deal primarily with private matters and hence may be indistinguishable from fully-fledged online diaries focused on personal issues; these have had their own convention since 2000.[11] The terminology itself is still in flux, and the words diary, journal and weblog are used indiscriminately by practitioners and commentators. The difference between the two forms is indeed becoming blurred and seems to depend mostly on the technology chosen to upload one's writings online.

Whether they are concerned with the private or the public sphere, weblogs are updated daily at the very least, and often two or three times a day, with entries appearing in reverse chronological order, the most recent one always being superadded on top of all the earlier ones. Many writers have added a blog alongside their online diary, either altogether leaving behind the diary to switch to a blog, like Shmuel, or keeping both, but using them for different purposes, like Aiyah or Sam Snyder. The latter   infrequently posts essay-length entries on specific subjects in his diary, while using his blog for his daily writings.[12] However, the distinction between diaries and weblogs is increasingly meaningless, as one form seems to have morphed into the other.

---

[8]   Glenn Reynolds is a law professor at the University of Tennessee http://www.instapundit.com/ . Accessed September 2003.
[9]   Rebecca Blood is both a blogger and the author of a manual about blogging, *The Weblog Handbook*, Perseus Publishing, 2002; *BoingBoing* is maintained by a collective of writers, http://boingboing.net. Accessed October 2001.
[10]   BlogCon, http://blogs.law.harvard.edu/bloggerCon/nutshell. Accessed September 2003.
[11]   JournalCon, http://www.journalcon.com/ . Accessed September 2003.
[12]   Sam Snyder's *Continuum,* May 22, 2003 journal entry. http://www.itwarren.com/continuum/2002may/05222002.shtml.

Diaries or weblogs are rarely uploaded online without a title. Often creative, the title either attempts to reflect the general tone of the body of text, or is the pseudonym of the writer. Titles are what Genette calls a threshold, both an indication as to what to expect from the text and an invitation to the reader. Alternatively, they may be an attempt at misleading readers or prodding them towards an interpretation (Genette 1987: 73-76). Then again, some titles have a definite intertextual element, harking back to the most hallowed *topoi*: *Confessions of an ADD Physics Major*, for instance, alludes to Saint Augustine and to his numerous followers, from Jean-Jacques Rousseau to Thomas de Quincey, to name but two of them.[13] Both diaries and weblogs possess sections enabling the self-introduction of the diarist, typically called an 'about' or a 'bio' section. Similar to the preface in print autobiographies, this section is primarily aimed at ensuring the proper interpretation of what is to follow (Genette 1987: 183). As shall become apparent in a later section, the incipit or preamble to a weblog or diary is far more than a purely descriptive exercise, and may in fact represent an authentic attempt at analysing and synthesizing the multiple meanings of self-representational writing, different from diary writing proper and its dailiness.

Diaries and weblogs also contain space for photo albums, a links section to other journals, an archive for past entries and a miscellany of more thematically ordered rubrics depending on the focus of each diarist. The division of each screen in three or more parts is often seen, and the large number of links both around and within the text turns each page into the threshold towards ever more content. Blogs and online diaries therefore give at the same time the impression of uniformity in their structures and endless diversity in their details.

2. A structural analysis of online diaries

A structural approach is one way of laying the groundwork for an aesthetic study of websites going beyond the individual characteristics of each to ascertain the features common to all. Such a treatment necessarily implies that, in a first stage, contents will be, if not overlooked, at least downplayed. The close textual analysis of individual diaries is hardly compatible with the identification of these

---

[13] ADD stands for attention deficit disorder. http://youngaddfemale.blogspot.com. Accessed April 2003.

writings' fundamental structures, which is the main focus of the present chapter.

Four such structural features can be identified and of these, the first one, accumulation, can be said to be the one characteristic all websites, be they private, political or commercial, have in common (Serfaty 2002a: 79). The additional characteristics are open-endedness, self-reflexivity and co-production.

2.1. Accumulation

Accumulation refers to the fact that text no longer is the only mode of expression for online diarists, who use the full gamut of media available to writers. Two or more media therefore appear side-by-side, with either merely ornamental or intentionally thematic purposes. Sometimes the coexistence is not actual but implied, as evidenced by the practice of providing links to pictures located outside the text proper. Hypertext links thus provide a kind of anaphoric allusion to unseen but potentially visible pictures.

2.1.1. Multimedia

Although text still remains the major medium in early diaries, more recent diaries include pictures of the writers as in Bunt Sign's diary or Terri's diary, pictures of pets, of the view out of the window (Bunt Sign), of the desk they write on (Shmuel), or wedding pictures.[14] Many such pictures were traditional snapshots, scanned and uploaded on the Internet. The mass diffusion of the digital camera has, however, given an entirely new momentum to the iconography in online diaries. Anything is deemed to be picture-worthy, be it a salad or a pair of sneakers used for jogging,[15] or particularly weird Christmas presents.[16] As we shall see in a later section, digital cameras enable a large number of self-portraits, especially given the longer time they take to snap, thanks to which diarists can strike a pose. Portraits taken with the camera held at arm's length abound, prolonging the time-honored

---

[14]   A sampling of early diaries can be consulted on *The Online Diary History Project*, http://www.diaryhistoryproject.com/recollections/1995_01_03.htm; see also Bunt Sign's Diary, http://www.buntsign.com/index.html; Terri's Diary *Footnotes*; http://www.secraterri.com; Shmuel's Diary http://www.babeltower.org/soapbox/blog/; Houston blogs, http://h-townblogs.blogspot.com/. Websites accessed November 2001 and *seq.*

[15]   Sam Snyder's weblog *Continuum*, *op. cit.* December 7, 2003 entry. Accessed December 2003.

[16]   *Dreaming Among the Jade Clouds*, December 17, 1998. http://www.jade-leaves.com/journal/98/12/j981217.shtml . Accessed November 2003.

practice of painters who painted their own reflection in a mirror. Because the pictures can be viewed on the camera's LCD screen as soon as they are snapped, the time hiatus between taking a picture and having it developed disappears; and because pictures can easily be transferred onto a computer and then uploaded online, it becomes easier to multiply representations of reality, no matter how trivial the subject.

In a more traditional vein, drawings and friezes representing leaves, flowers, insects such as ladybugs or bees, reminiscent of the notebooks with lock and key traditionally given to girls to write their diary in, also show up regularly on both men's and women's sites.[17] Some diarists use their own drawings, often bespeaking undeniable graphic talent, like Medea Sin or Al Schroeder.[18] Less frequently but significantly, the diarist's voice can be heard on audio files, as for Shmuel or Kymm.[19] Webcams can sometimes be found in some diaries, for instance in Medea Sin's, but this is an infrequent occurrence, as the real focus of such personal narratives is writing. Medea Sin himself only provides a view of his head at a three-quarter angle. Ads for software or in some cases for sponsors can be found at the bottom of the page, but the examples are also few and far between, the only logo found with any degree of consistency being that of the webring the diary may be affiliated with.

2.1.2. Linking

All of the diaries, even the most plainly designed, include hypertext links to various sites, to other diaries, to fiction written by the author and to a seemingly infinite number of texts, generating an impression of boundless content.[20] Linking is of course not random. A blogger who realizes someone has linked to his/her site often responds by also linking to his reader's blog, in a self- and reciprocal

---

[17] http://www.inu.org/alewife/index.htm; http://ladybug.notsweet.net/. Websites accessed February 2002 and *seq.*

[18] Medea Sin, http://www.medeasin.com/jindex.htm; Al Schroeder's *NovaNotes*, http://www.novanotes.com . Accessed November 2001.

[19] "Honors and Multimedia", *Shmuel's Soapbox*, March 18, 2000. http://www.babeltower.org/soapbox/0300/031800.html; "Only pussies use Html editors", *The Mighty Kymm*, August 2, 1996, http://www.sweetasabiscuit.com/mightykymm/1996/august/080296.html . Sites accessed September 2001 and *seq.*

[20] http://www.mamohanraj.com/Diary/diary.html; http://carolyn.org/writings.html. Websites accessed December 2001 and *seq.*

promotional process that has been characterized as "the incestuous, snowballing sensation of getting linked in the blogosphere" (Glaser 2003: 87). For some commentators like Jay Rosen, head of New-York University's School of Journalism, this practice is fundamentally conservative in the sense that it relies on the traditional means of creating and preserving journalistic standards: "Weblogs deal in the golden rule, modified to read: link unto others as you would have them link unto you" (Rosen 2003). Yet this view does not do justice to the richness and variety of linking procedures in online blogs and diaries, in part as a result of software capabilities. Linking indeed is not only done towards the sites of friends or of bloggers one would like to befriend; linking also occurs whenever the diarist wants to point to explanatory contents on the Web as well as whenever diarists wants to direct the reader towards older entries or photo albums within their own diary. The latter practice makes the hypertextual link very similar to a footnote with, however, a major difference. Where traditional footnotes are static, hypertextual links are dynamic and can potentially lead the reader, link after link, to the infiniteness of the Net's contents. Therefore inward-looking hypertextual links which at first sight might seem to be self-contained, or even solipsistic, in fact energize online diaries and conceivably connect them to the entirety of the online world.

Linking moreover is very often done under the heading "other diaries I read", showing that no matter how personal self-representational writing may be, it relates to other writings of a similar kind, in a vast movement toward intertextuality. In keeping with the general Netiquette in force in diarists' webrings, none of the links provided are objects of criticism or rejection. Only valued diaries appear in the links list, and if a comment is included, it is invariably laudatory.

Accumulation strategies indeed seem to be typical of Internet sites, apparently out of sheer joy and enthusiasm about the technological feats made possible by the Internet; as a result of their use, the space of Internet diaries seems to be literally saturated. This drive towards comprehensiveness, however, points to several layers of meaning. Accumulation first meets the need for exhaustiveness felt by diary writers. Eager as they are to disclose themselves to the full and aware at the same time of the Sisyphean impossibility of the task, they multiply the angles of approach and attempt all-inclusiveness. As a result, they keep accumulating details about an event or a state of mind, coming back to the same point and trying to unravel its meaning, no matter how minute it might seem, piling up photographs upon drawings, using punctuation erratically in an attempt at enhancing its expressiveness.

Accumulation of information through the use of different media is also an attempt at creating a rounded character, in Forsterian terms, as opposed to the flat bi-dimensionality and rigid order imposed by print on a blank page (Forster 1963: 75). Diaries thus endeavour to produce a complex, multi-faceted fictional self or *persona*, a point I shall return to in more detail in the following section.

Further, the accumulation of different media made possible by diaries frees them from the constraints of form and style, which leads to absolute freedom of representation and to the destabilization of a unified vision of personality. Online diaries provide a space to accumulate signs in so that daily life and states of mind can unfold in all their chaotic complexity. The accumulation of signs counters the comforting simplifications of everyday life to point to the radical singularity, the absolute uniqueness and the endless complexity of a given individual – traits that are supposed to be downplayed in day-to-day social interactions, in which one has to sustain one's image as a public character, whom others expect to behave in certain, stereotypical ways.

In addition, the reader or viewer must perceive and make sense of disparate data provided through diverse media (print, photographs, videos, audio files), in an ongoing process of interpretation and construction of meaning. Yet, no matter how dissimilar the sources may be, each piece of information bolsters every other piece and conveys mutually reinforcing information. Accumulation thus creates density and texture. Signs are piled upon signs and their very multiplicity is conducive to the production of meaning. Accumulation fulfils the all-important function of immersing the viewer into the world picture of the diary writer and requiring him to interpret the material provided him. This is the first, albeit minimal, aspect of the interactivity characterizing online diaries. It is a bid for "total participation", in which reading is akin to "the active appropriation of the Other" (Kristeva 1969: 120).

2.1.3. Online diaries and the written word

Traditional diaries have had a special relationship with the written word inasmuch as writing lends them several of its characteristics. By the spatialization of the spoken word it affords (Ong 1982), writing makes possible the structuring of self-description and ultimately the structuring of self, even in the midst of the chaotic complexity mentioned earlier. Moreover, the permanence of the written word lends itself to a diachronic vision of the self. Interestingly, even online, where multiple media coexist, writing retains its primacy, albeit under a very specific guise, i.e. the fragment. Because entries are necessarily separated by each day's date, each entry is hemmed in by all others, yet remains discrete, fragmentary. The relation between each entry need not be stated, because it will have to be established by the reader or by the diarist who revises his/her own text. The temporal sequence of entries is predicated upon this blank or interval between two fragments which, no matter how close to one another their date shows them to be, still remain silent about a myriad events in the diarist's life. Even Amiel's seventeen thousand pages still fall short of telling it all. The blanks between fragmented entries make it possible for the diarists to invent the thread that will be likely to reconnect the disparate facets of their lives over the long term. Dating each entry is therefore not only a way of visualizing the passage of time, but also a way of subjectively experiencing it.

Heterogeneity due to fragmentation, then, is the hallmark of the kind of writing specific to diaries. Diaries also bear the mark of heterogeneity in that they very often encompass different media, in addition to writing. As we saw above, pictures, drawings and sometimes even audio files are produced alongside the written text. These insertions tend to interrupt the linear unfolding of the text, in two different ways: first, by introducing pictures of the writer or of landscapes, often with an explanatory caption, they add a new, external scene to the inner scene the writing delineates. Thus pictures accentuate the need for yet more explanations, interpretations, yet more writing. Pictures constitute another system of signs that reifies the body, turns it into the Other, and requires from diarists a further investment in the written word if they are to make sense of themselves.

In addition, when pictures of family members or of friends are introduced, the accompanying explanations inject somebody else's life into the diarist's text. The online diary is no longer a text enclosed within the confines of a single person's life, but a text open to all the vagaries of interrelationships.

Not only does the introduction of pictures or sounds produce heterogeneity, it also multiplies borders: borders between text and images, images and captions, downloaded mp3 files and text. These multiple borders induce an effect of hybridization between different media, not so much because they merge into each other, but because their mere juxtaposition prevents the construction of a unified, linear, ordered portrait of the self while simultaneously creating new meanings and opening up new spaces for interpretations defying the control of the diarists themselves.

2.2. Closure vs. open-endedness

Two sorts of diaries can be found on the Net: some are limited to a pre-set period of time, such as *Charlie's Daily Web*, which was planned to last for exactly a year and stopped at the appointed time, or Carolyn Burke's diary which was posted from 1995 to 2001. Other diaries actually started in the seventies in the traditional way, were coded into HTML and uploaded online, and are still regularly updated, like Terri's *Footnotes* or *Jimsjournal* [sic], among many others.[21] These two forms reproduce the traditional distinction between autobiography and diary writing.

As I indicated in the introduction, autobiographies are self-contained forms. Diaries, by contrast, are basically open-ended; they are usually started with no clear idea of the time when they are going to end. Linearity is the distinguishing feature of their enunciative pattern, through the inclusion of a date and of rigorously chronological entries. Self-representation in diaries also differs markedly, veering more towards self-expression than the production of a consistent, unified version of oneself: in this case as well, open-endedness is the rule. In addition, diaries being ostensibly private texts, they can be seen as a means to think through the seam between the private and the public self and as such, they are more attuned to contemporary uncertainties about the self. Ever since Gusdorf's groundbreaking 1956 essay, studies of self-representational writing have rested on the assumption that the selves which emerge in diaries come into being through the writing process itself and hence do not necessarily reflect the writer's actual experience. Diaries thus construct a fiction of self (Gusdorf 1956; Benstock 1988; Eakin 1991; Harel 1997).

---

[21] Jimsjournal [sic] started in 1996 and Carolyn Burke's Journal started in 1995 and is now offline. Both are part of the *Online Diary History Project*: http://www.diaryhistoryproject.com/; Terri's Diary *op. cit.*; Charlie's Daily Web http://www.geocities.com/SunsetStrip/9652/report.html. Websites accessed December 2001 and *seq.*

It appears at first sight that the distinction between diaries and autobiographies becomes more nebulous on the Internet because the continuing online presence of these texts gives rise to phenomena such as a discussion list, for Carolyn Burke's diary, or messages in a guest book or plain e-mail messages, all of which afford finite texts a degree of open-endedness.[22] The autobiographical genre seems to fade into the diaristic genre, in a process of hybridization often observable on the Internet. Yet it soon becomes apparent that the most attractive blogs and diaries are the ones updated on a daily and sometimes hourly basis. The graphic representation of the passage of time thus provided is one of their drawing powers. It is precisely this open-endedness which gives online self-representational writing its fascinating, sometimes even addictive quality. The reader's interest is kept up by the discontinuity and the irregularity inherent in daily entries, as well as by the constantly deferred promise of an ending, of closure. Open-endedness is both a defining feature of online diaries and one of the reasons for their success.

In addition, online diaries are characterized by dialectics of stability and motion. The linear chronological entries over months or years, the excruciatingly detailed descriptions of the trivia of everyday life or the painful soul-searching engaged in day in, day out provide a space for stability, fixity even. Yet the fixed framework set up in this way allows each diarist a space of freedom in which to write using the first-person singular, the pronoun " I ". As diarists write " I ", they have to work out a definition of self that is the very first step towards self-transformation, open-ended and potentially infinite. The writing process itself creates this space of redefinition: " the intention of self-representational writing [...] is a dynamic factor in the evolution of the mind's reality. Scrutinizing identity contributes to constituting identity" (Gusdorf 1991a: 11).[23]

This is compounded by a practice common to many Internet diaries, a link to the entry of the year before ("One year ago") or to the following years ("One year from now") and by the presence of archives. The two devices – flashback and foreshadowing – provide both the reader and the writer of diaries with a long-term vision and with a sense of perspective. Looking back, the road travelled can be

---

[22]   This discussion list contains 136 messages and stopped being active in September 2001. http://groups.yahoo.com/group/clburke/messages. Accessed February 2002.
[23]   "L'intention des écritures du moi [...] intervient comme un facteur dynamique dans l'évolution de la réalité mentale. L'interrogation d'identité contribue à la constitution de l'identité".

measured, the self-transformation or lack of it can be gauged - and the fragmentation of life into a myriad trivia can be bypassed and transmuted into a narrative of selfhood, an archaeological reconstruction of the 'I'.

It is essential to realize that this coherence is a retroactive, constantly evolving reconstruction. Freud pointed out the fact, sustained by the findings of Einsteinian physics, that the passage of time is a comfortable illusion, that the past, the present and the future are but beliefs. Past events are not gone, they coexist with present experience and their continued impact appears in dreams, which collapse our habitual notions of time. In a way, self-representational writing does the same thing when presenting diarists with all their entries on the same plane, merely separated by the entry date, thus countering our intuitive perception of time. The synchronous co-presence of entries quite literally illustrates the fact that past events co-exist with present ones in human consciousness. Accordingly, the individual's constant interpretive process is what gives consistency and symbolic weight to the past, because there is no such thing as an over-and-done-with incident for human memory. Open-endedness therefore is both a pre-requisite for and a by-product of diaristic writing.

2.3. Self-reflexivity

Self-reflexivity takes two major forms: commentaries about the Internet, and commentaries about diary-writing itself. Throughout the various diaries under examination, the writers indeed all ask themselves why they have taken up diary writing.

Such comments are very often found in the incipit to the diary proper, but hardly ever in later entries. Lejeune indeed states that "the beginning of a diary is nearly always emphasized. People seldom begin without saying so. The new writing territory is staked out in one way or another" (Lejeune 2000a: 209).[24] These pre-texts can be seen as guidelines to the reader, as tools to pilot and sometimes control the addressee's interpretation of the diaristic narrative. The analysis of the diarists' motivation and writing process is so often located in the preamble to the diary proper that it might also have an "inchoative

---

[24] "Le début d'un journal est presque toujours souligné: il est rare qu'on commence sans le dire; on marque d'une manière ou d'une autre ce nouveau territoire d'écriture".

function, akin to a warm-up" (Simonet-Tenant 2001: 90),[25] contributing to clarifying the goals of the diarists and their relationships with their prospective readers. In the process, diarists produce an elaborate meta-discourse.

2.3.1. Modernity

Numerous writers marvel at the vistas of opportunity opened by the Internet for "community-building" or for achieving world peace.[26] An early practitioner writes: "If each of us were to catalog our own human experience and make it available on the web, we could lend to each other an omnipotence unattainable prior to the existence of the Net".[27] Such remarks – deemed utopian by the very people making them – bespeak at the same time a degree of belief in technological determinism and an awareness of the modernity of the Net. Online diarists perceive themselves as pioneers, consciously engaging in the development of a new set of practices. This is why they feel the need to think through both the Internet's future and their own online experience. Self-reflexivity about the Internet is thus a means of joining a fellowship of cutting-edge practitioners of a cutting-edge art.

In a more down-to-earth strain, many welcome the sheer accessibility of the medium. Ladybug, for instance, is maintaining a long-distance relationship and wants to " let her boy-friend into her little garden of thoughts and feelings and observations".[28] Miriam similarly writes about "business travel […], restaurants in Boulder, Colorado, random factoids, the deaths of obscure celebrities".[29] It is only indirectly, when she lists her life's goals, for instance, that she attempts more than a purely descriptive entry.[30]Both are highly aware of the public nature of their writings and they accordingly construct a narrative that has very little to do with their inner being; their text is, ostensibly at least, an eminently social activity.

---

[25] "Le métadiscours […] remplit une fonction inchoative et serait l'équivalent d'une mise en voix".
[26] Carolyn Burke, http://carolyn.org/Page6.html. Accessed February 2002; Mary Anne's *Ongoing, Erratic Diary*, http://www.mamohanraj.com/Diary/whyjourn.html. Accessed February 2002 and *seq.*
[27] Diane Patterson, http://www.spies.com/~diane/ , quoted by Open Pages, http://www.hedgehog.net/op/references.html . Accessed December 2001.
[28] http://ladybug.notsweet.net/archives/2001_05.php. Accessed February 2002.
[29] http://www.areasofunrest.net/faq.html. Accessed February 2002.
[30] http://www.areasofunrest.net/lifelist.html. Accessed February 2002.

2.3.2. The art of the diary

The potential for creating a new art form frequently appears in the diarists' statements of intent. In the following example, the diarist analyzes the formal potentialities of public self-representational writing:

> Not to sound all academic-y (rhymes with gimmicky), but I think web journals are an incredibly fascinating form. They have their conventions, and some of the greats know just when and how to break those conventions to breathtaking effect. The speed of publication, the interaction with readers, the courage it takes to put some raw thoughts up there and *leave* them there, long after you're ashamed of them--these things are new. [...] But that's my point. This is an art form, here.[31]

This meta-discourse demonstrates the writer's awareness both of the generic features online journals share with traditional ones and of the kinship between diary writing and fiction. Another diarist, Jessamyn,[32] titles her diary *Internet Persona*, underscoring the fictional and theatrical element in the representation of self built up over hundreds of entries. Terri states that her journal, *Footnotes*, is "a hybrid of observation and perception ... detail and overview ... disclosure and omission. I don't tell you everything, in other words. I don't think I have to. And not everything I *do* tell you is 100% factual, 100% of the time ... there is literal account of fact ... and there is gentle manipulation of fact for the sake of art".[33] The diarist's definition of her craft could not be further from any claim to artlessness or spontaneity. She is consciously espousing well-established practises of composition and revision; her use of the word "art" points to her awareness that, in converting experience into discourse, she is creating a fiction which will tend to "lean towards acknowledged literary forms [...] requiring a familiarity with and an interest in literary forms" (Kagle, Gramegna 1996: 39).

Terri's statement about the elusiveness of truth and its relationship with art pinpoints the chasm between diaristic narratives and the raw rendering of day-to-day experience. Online diarists indeed make it a

---

[31] *Subsequent Events*, http://www.amyd.org/about.html . Accessed December 2002.

[32] *Internet Persona,* http://jessamyn.diary-x.com/journal.cgi?entry=200009191335. Accessed September 2003.

[33] Terri's Diary, *Footnotes,* http://www.secraterri.com/bio.html; emphasis in the text. Accessed February 2002.

point not to upload a sloppily written text. Like one of their most famous forebears, Samuel Pepys, they revise their entries and carefully edit their own writing. This puts to rest what Rosenwald calls the myth of the diary's artlessness, or the idea that diary entries are written quickly and without revisions (Rosenwald 1988: 21).

In addition, all of the diarists have a post-modern awareness of previous diaries, journals they borrow from more or less consciously. Self-reflexivity is a function of the modern use of intertextuality, i.e. the inclusion, in one's own writing, of existing literary models. This can be seen in the way diarists refer to the standard patterns they know they have to abide by. Thus, diarists sometimes, either consciously or unconsciously, resort to some of the most hallowed diaristic formulas. When each entry closes with "pillow time" (Sam Snyder) or "I'm out" (Ayiah), for instance, the phrases are strongly reminiscent of Samuel Pepys' "and so to bed" punctuating most entries (Rosenwald 1988: 19). Online diaries can therefore be said to be the representation of inner spaces as well as of the self-consciousness of the post-modern writer, for whom writing primarily is an exploration of the system of signs constituting language.

2.3.3. Self-justification

Self-reflexivity may also have defensive functions. Diarists feel the need to justify their involvement in this practice, probably because it no longer enjoys the religious and/or cultural sanction it used to possess in the past. Upholding online self-representational writing may also turn out to be necessary given the attacks it has had to weather since it came into existence. In a violent rant, an author thus writes, in what amounts to an attempt at shaming diarists into silence:

> I find many on-line journals frightening, all the more so because graphomania is not just an isolated phenomenon; no, it is a *cultural ethos and a morality*, and it is not restricted to writing *per se*. On the contrary, it pervades the very fabric of our every-day relations with others. [...] We may see graphomania as the overpowering conflation of the will to truth, the will to power, and ressentiment. The on-line personal journal [is] at its worst, a new outlet for personal refuge we would otherwise find inane, petty, and grotesquely self-indulgent. [...] The gnomic injunction of your average on-line journal is two-fold and interpellative: Confess, and be true

to your Self (understood here as something essential and virtuous). (Napolitano 1996).[34]

This is a modern expression of an ancient prohibition against self-talk. Blaise Pascal's "hateful I" is still internalised by many who scorn the self-scrutiny, let alone the potential for publicity, online diaries enable. This is obvious in many ways. A diarists' webring, for instance, calls its members "escribitionists"[35] and the same word is used by a diarist describing his own work[36] – the strongly pathological connotations of this coinage being apparently embraced by the very practitioners of the form. None of this contempt fortunately stops committed bloggers or diarists from writing about their lives at length on the Internet everyday, and trying to think through the various issues raised in the process. Online diarists need to think about their writing even while they project themselves into it. Self-reflexivity therefore enables both writing and the critical distancing from that writing which is crucial to the slow construction of meaning diarists are engaged in.

2.3.3.1. From flippancy to earnestness

The answers provided by diarists when attempting to unravel their motivations vary in form but hardly ever in content. The flippant "Why not ?" Shmuel or Mary-Anne begin with is always followed by a more elaborate attempt at making the author's intentions clear. The motivations of diarists often appear to be quite intricate. Mary Anne thus starts out by saying that she is keeping a diary so that her acquaintances and family will be able to keep up with her, relieving her of the chore of correspondence. A few lines down, however, she admits to editing the journal quite a bit; she refrains from overly personal details, yet has been helped get over rough patches in her life by readers and by her own writings. Finally she acknowledges the fact that as a writer, she has "a desire to be known and understood and speak [her] truth and have others listening, responding, touched".[37] Another English literature major and budding writer, Shmuel, finds the experience valuable to "work out a few philosophical and

---

[34] A more balanced critique, written by an online diarist, attempts to define standards for online journals: Diane Patterson, 'Why Web Journals Suck: An Essay'. http://www.nobody-knows-anything.com/websuck.html . Accessed December 2001.
[35] Diarist Net Registry, http://diarist.net/registry/ . Accessed December 2001.
[36] Shmuel's Soapbox, *op. cit.*, September 29, 1999 entry. Accessed September 2001.
[37] http://www.mamohanraj.com/Diary/whyjourn.html. Accessed February 2002.

psychological issues" and hopes that "having an audience will keep [him] going".[38] Unlike these two diarists, who are still in their twenties, Doug Franklin is a middle-aged man who writes: "I've always wanted to be a writer. [...] I was in the wrong clique to get into journalism [...]. Then my brother [...] got into it in a big way. [...] He won a Pulitzer [....] and there is no way I could compete with him. Nor do I want to. However, I still have this itch that can only be alleviated by writing something".[39] Jessamyn, another diarist, states:

> I have always liked to write. [...] And Mom may not know this part, but I've always imagined I was famous. I've given oh so many Oscar acceptance speeches. From approximately ages 8 to 15, every moment of my life was part of a tv [sic] show or movie (when I went to the bathroom, I'd try to make sure the folks watching at home didn't get a glimpse of anything they shouldn't be seeing). I've given countless interviews to magazines like *Cosmo* and *Rolling Stone* and *People.* [...] The thing is, I can't write songs. [...] But I can write this. I don't pretend to think that everyone likes (or would like) the way I write or the things I write about. I don't expect to be famous because of this journal. [...] But *I* like what I'm writing. And I do expect that some of you will read something I've written, and that some of you will FEEL something because of what you've read. Because of what I've written. And that motivates me.[40]

These excerpts all illustrate the same need to justify and validate diary writing by one's calling, one's affinities with the writer's craft. While Mary Anne is a published author and Shmuel an aspiring one, and can therefore hope to become full-time writers, Doug Franklin and Jessamyn are aware of the impossibility of such a goal, and their words acquire some poignancy, further emphasized by the quickly denied hint of sibling rivalry in Doug Franklin's case. All quite clearly, albeit humorously, refer to the need for love, acceptance and contact that is at the heart of exposing one's writings for others to read. Jessamyn relates this to a childish urge to be famous – fame being nothing but a metonymy for a universal demand for love that merely takes on different forms as time goes by. As we shall see in a

---

[38]   http://www.babeltower.org/soapbox/why.html. Accessed February 2002.
[39]   'Why am I doing an on-line journal ?' http://nilknarf.net/stuff/why2.htm.
[40]   Jessamyn's *Internet Persona.*
http://jessamyn.diary-x.com/journal.cgi?entry=200009191335 . Emphasis in the text.
Accessed December 2001.

later section, the urge to be recognized and connect with others is a crucial motivation for all diarists and webloggers.

Whatever their ultimate purpose, however, all take writing seriously   and hence feel the need to highlight the significance of diaristic writing to ward off the charge of futility, navel-gazing and irrelevance diarists have long been the butt of. Such a strategy may also enable them to evade the inescapable realization that "any learned or naïve meditation about one's own life ends up in a perception of obscene meaninglessness" (de Mijolla-Mellor 1990: 104).[41] The feeling of vacuity must therefore be transcended both for the writer and the implied or actual reader. Writing thus becomes a way of taming the formlessness of experience, a formlessness which prefigures that of death.

2.3.3.2. The diary as a quest for truth

Another such text, the incipit to a diary entitled *'Documented life'*, introduces a different idea. The diarist is Miles Hochstein, a social scientist in his early forties, whose site presents an interesting mix of autobiographical and diaristic features. Using forty-five pictures of himself on his front page, each one introducing more pictures of himself and family members with some captions, this diarist traces his forebears over several generations and arrives at the present day, without, however, wrapping up his story, since he leaves space for more pictures, up to the year 2049. In this way, the open-endedness of his site links it to diaristic forms, even though very few everyday life notations appear. In his preamble, Miles Hochstein sets forth his reasons for creating his diary and posting it online. The author begins by stating that he is "dedicated to getting the facts right", but qualifies this in the next paragraph when he adds: "I have not tried to tell every truth and even for those truths I do tell, perfect objectivity has not been my goal. It is enough for me to avoid serious misrepresentations. [...] The photographs help keep me honest".[42] Revealing oneself while at the same time avoiding total exposure constitutes one of the difficulties each writer of the self has to contend with.

Miles Hochstein's statement of intent is also an example of the so-called autobiographical compact which, according to Lejeune, is

---

[41]   "L'obscène absence de sens sur laquelle débouche toute méditation savante ou naïve concernant sa propre existence".

[42]   *Documented Life: An Autodocumentary*, http://www.documentedlife.com/welcome.htm. Accessed September 2003.

entered into by each diarist: "Unlike all forms of fiction, biographies and autobiographies are *referential* texts: just like scientific or historical discourse, they claim they are providing information on a reality that is external to the text" (Lejeune 1975: 36).[43] For Lejeune, what really matters is not so much the way in which the diarist carries out what he has set out to do, but the very fact that the pact was made and adhered to. In the passage under consideration here, the very wording indeed indicates that the diarist is aware of the fundamental fallacy of any attempt at achieving full transparency. From the outset, the diarist hints at his awareness of the fact that truth is a construct. Miles Hochstein's paradoxical stance, combining his striving for accuracy and his simultaneous realization that truth is unattainable, locates him at the very hub of the ironies of self-representational writing.

In addition, Miles Hochstein's reliance on pictures, so typical of Internet diaries, appears charged with meaning. A documentary function is clearly ascribed to pictures which are supposed to act as pieces of evidence bolstering the statements of the author, and this particular belief in the honesty of pictures seems to be taken at face-value. Yet throughout his diary, Miles is taken aback by the strangeness of some pictures of himself at an earlier age. In the following passage, for instance, he comments on the year 1986; the fact that he does so in dialogical form seems to indicate the inherently ambivalent results of the urge to chronicle oneself, inasmuch as it ends up confronting the diarist with discarded versions of self, hence giving rise to some unease, perhaps even threatening his current definition of himself and forcing him to confront the uncertainty inherent in any personal narrative:

> *Question*: So you don't like what you see in this photo and document?
> *Answer*: I remember what it felt like, and it seems like a sad time, a cul de sac. There was no apparent way to move my life forward. Something had to change, and soon. But at this moment the future was almost completely obscure.
> *Question*: Is that the whole truth?

---

[43] "Par opposition à toutes les formes de fiction, la biographie et l'autobiographie sont des textes *référentiels*: exactement comme le discours scientifique ou historique, ils prétendent apporter une information sur une 'réalité' extérieure au texte". Emphasis in the text.

> *Answer*: The truth is never whole. It is always fragments of broken pottery that lie scattered across the floor, waiting to be reassembled. (*Documented Life*: 1986)

Pictures appear to turn him into the Other, and his sense of bewilderment actually causes him to unleash a flood of words, thus belying the transparency of representation pictures are supposed to enable. Pictures resist interpretation, they introduce heterogeneity in diaristic discourse and so they lead to a proliferation of words (Kofman 1985: 24-29) which actually cover up more than they reveal. What they cover up is the split between self and modes of representation – a split conducive to the production of text, a text which in turn becomes the enigmatic metaphor of self.

2.4. Co-production

Whenever a diary writer edits or otherwise revises entries, "these superficially private writings become unmistakably public documents, intended for an external readership" (Bloom 1996: 23). Not only do all of the online diarists under consideration carefully polish their texts, they also provide enough background to help the reader identify the various characters interacting with the diary writer, thus contextualizing each entry. For instance, Carolyn Burke includes a list of "cast members", while Kevin includes a "cast list" subtitled "dramatis personae", thus further emphasizing the intertextuality and literariness of such writings.[44]

Readership is an important issue for all the diary writers in our sample. All of them include a link to their mailbox and avowedly relish responses from readers. All diaries feature a "Notify List", in which the diarist offers to e-mail readers whenever a new entry is uploaded. Weblogs push interactivity even further by including an answer button that automatically records and adds up the number of comments triggered by any given entry. Readers can thus see at a glance which entries have aroused the most interest. Terri expresses a general feeling when she writes in her introduction: " I crave feedback, I live for feedback".[45]

What all of this points to is that where traditional diaries were written for an implied, ideal reader, online diaries explicitly search for

---

[44] Carolyn Burke's diary, *op. cit*. Kevin's diary, *Change Over Time,* http://kevin.diary-x.com/?entry=castlist

[45] Terri's Diary, *op. cit,* "Biostuff". Accessed September 2001. This formulation has recently been revised and now reads: "I welcome feedback".

an audience and in so doing, turn themselves into a collaborative project. The interactions between writer and audience turn the diary into a process of co-production and co-enunciation (Chanfrault-Duchet 2000: 62; Foot, Schneider 2002: 23).

Moreover, reading diaries also turns into a creative process which interweaves with and modifies the diary itself, making it the center of a collective production of meaning through the fictionalization of the self and of the events in the writer's daily life. Diary writers create themselves as the central characters in a fictional theater populated by a large supporting cast of minor characters and of readers. The fiction thus created is essentially interactive and as such, thoroughly renews the art of the diary by turning it into a collaborative effort.

In both cases, however, the interaction with the audience gains such considerable importance because, while ostensibly working so hard at convincing others of the righteousness of their cause or of their actions, diarists are first and foremost working very hard at convincing themselves. And in this task, the audience plays the part of the looking glass which, by reflecting the diarist, institutes him or her as a separate individual through the signifying articulation of discourse and as an effect of language.

Co-production also points to the suffering caused by the difficulty of constructing oneself as a unified person (de Mijolla-Mellor 1990: 112). The feedback of readers is therefore required in order to reinforce the sense of the diarist's own identity. Each response to an entry gives diarists confirmation of their own existence. Identity construction is thus grounded in "inter-subjectivity " and is no longer confined to interiority (Jackson 1990: 140).

Co-production is inextricably linked with self-reflexivity inasmuch as the latter constitutes in part a thinking through of the issue of inter-subjectivity and hence of communication. In order for diarists to communicate their feelings and states of mind, they have to pre-suppose the existence of a common ground with others; in other words, they have to give up some of the uniqueness they have been working so hard to sustain through their writing. Overcoming the solipsistic closure into the self and reaching out to others implies giving up the solitude of the individual and instituting readers as the Other, whose very otherness, because it is irreducible, institutes the 'I' in return. In other words, the 'I' exists precisely because it relates to a 'You' and hence turns into a 'We'. Yet in no way is this a negation of individuality. What it amounts to is an optimistic belief in the capacity of diaristic writing *and* reading to bridge the gap between separate individuals. In addition, as we shall see in the following chapter, it is a way of setting out to think through the relationship between the individual and society, in a bid to compel the acceptance of uniqueness and somewhat abate the stringency of the injunction towards conformity. That joining society entails a recognition of one's irreducible separateness from it is not the least of the many ironies raised by online diaristic writing.

Chapter Two

Social Functions of Online Diaries in America

1. Connections

The fascination with online diaries, while not an exclusively American phenomenon, nevertheless appears to have elective affinities with some traits of American culture, both in terms of sheer numbers and because the social practice of diary-writing harks back to deeply entrenched undercurrents in American culture. The results of a Google search for online diaries written in French shows that the ratio to diaries written in English is of one to roughly 36.5, with an overwhelming majority of North Americans.[1] The largest diarists' webring thus lists 4,734 diaries written in the United States as opposed to 405 diaries originating from the United Kingdom and 28 from France.[2] An obvious explanation for this situation is suggested by the vastly superior number of American households connected to the Internet. Current estimates put Internet access at sixty percent of all households in the United States, totalling 149 million users, as compared to 33 million British users, while French Internet users add up to a mere 11 million.[3] Access to broadband Internet connections is far higher in the United States than in Europe. Such widespread access

---

[1]   The search for diaries in French used the keywords "journaux intimes" and restricted the search to France; the search engine retrieved 5,890 items. For a search using the keywords "online diaries" and conducted on the entire Web, the search engine retrieved 210,000 items. Search conducted on December 2002.

[2]   Source: Diarist.Net Registry. http://www.diarist.net/registry/. Accessed December 2002.

[3]   Source: Cyberatlas. *Global Online Populations.* March 2002.
http://cyberatlas.Internet.com/big_picture/geographics/article/0,1323,5911_151151,00.html. Accessed December 2002.

accounts for an ever more sophisticated use of the Internet in the United States of America, according to a survey carried out in March 2002 by the Pew Internet and American Life Project detailing daily online activities. The survey shows that one percent of all American users "create a web log or "blog" that others can read online".[4] The rapid diffusion of technological innovation is indeed a recurrent feature of American civilization, spurred on by large-scale public policies encouraging and developing their use. As regards the Internet, one of the most important measures voted by the Clinton administration in 1996 was the e-rate, a tax on every local or long distance phone call meant to finance low-cost Internet access in public places such as schools, libraries or hospitals.[5] By the end of President Clinton's second term, 95% of all schools and 65% of all hospitals were connected to the Internet. This policy was pursued and expanded by the Bush administration, showing that support for technology is an essentially bi-partisan issue.

Yet familiarity with technology and with the Internet, while a prerequisite, still provides only a surface explanation and falls far short of accounting for the phenomenon of online diaries and their success in the United States. A deeper set of causes, having to do with the American philosophical tradition, may underlie the rise of the blogging phenomenon and more generally of online diary-writing. The practice of keeping an online diary may indeed be seen as a direct offshoot of the philosophical outlook developed in America in the nineteenth century, Transcendentalism.

2. The influence of Emerson

Emerson's philosophy of the individual has been shown to be essential to the development and articulation of the American construct of national identity, turning Transcendentalism into the most far-reaching intellectual movement of the nineteenth century (Laugier 2002: 57). Two of Emerson's essays, "Self-Reliance" and "The American Scholar", are especially relevant to online diary-writing. In addition, keeping a journal was a nearly lifelong practice for Emerson himself, providing a precious template of social attitudes towards diaristic practises in nineteenth century America.

---

[4] Source: *The Pew Internet and American Life Project.*
http://www.pewInternet.org/reports/chart.asp?img=Daily_A6.htm. Accessed December 2002.
[5] http://congress.nw.dc.us/e-rate Accessed September 2001.

"Self-Reliance," Emerson's 1841 essay, charts the difficulty human beings come up against when attempting to create themselves as subjects:

> Society everywhere is in conspiracy against the manhood of every one of its members. Society is a joint-stock company, in which the members agree, for the better securing of his bread to each shareholder, to surrender the liberty and culture of the eater. The virtue in most request is conformity. Self-reliance is its aversion. It loves not realities and creators, but names and customs. (...) Whoso would be a man, must be a nonconformist. He who would gather immortal palms must not be hindered by the name of goodness, but must explore if it be goodness. Nothing is at last sacred but the integrity of your own mind. Absolve you to yourself, and you shall have the suffrage of the world. (Emerson 1841). [6]

When contrasting conformity with self-reliance, Emerson insists on the persistence of conflict within the subject between authority, conformity and self-creation, even while affirming the need for self-creation. Emerson therefore institutes the creation of the self as the locus of a tug-of-war between opposites, having nothing to do with an ideal self but rather being a constant process of becoming (Cavell 1996: 302; Domenach 2002: 98). Such an approach necessarily entails giving great importance to the inscription of this process within one's activities and one's relationship with the world at large. Diaristic writing, as exemplified in Emerson's voluminous *Journals*, provides space for just such an inscription (Gilman 1960-1982).

2.1. Emerson's *Journals*

Emerson first started his *Notebooks* by following John Locke's recommendations for commonplace books, which were supposed to contain quotes from one's readings or the transient thoughts one felt were worth recording, thus providing material for future writing. The real originality of Locke's method was the indexing method it suggested so as to enable future reference (Rosenwald 1988: 36). Having consciously set out to abide by Locke's rules, Emerson then proceeded to intersperse his commonplace book with all manner of private data. This is due to the fact that he was influenced by another tradition, that of the Puritan journal of spiritual progress, as

---

[6] Ralph Waldo Emerson, *Essays: First Series.* Project Gutenberg. http://www.ibiblio.org/gutenberg/etext01/1srwe10.txt. Accessed December 2002.

exemplified by his aunt's Mary Moody Emerson's journal (Rosenwald 1988: 36). In other words, Emerson fused the diaristic form and the commonplace book (Rosenwald 1988: 58). In so doing, by the mere chronological juxtaposition of excerpts from the books he had been reading and autobiographical material, Emerson gave a glimpse of the individual wrestling with creativity that characterizes the Transcendentalist artist and his vision of the foundation of value within the self. Lawrence Rosenwald argues that this attitude is specifically American:

> Emerson has chosen to put in his book not only the thousand scraps of reading and writing a commonplace book must contain but also those contingent data it must exclude. Or: Emerson has chosen to put in his diary not only the continuous record of his life and thought but also the thousand evanescent thoughts by which that record is complicated. In his book, that is, the private and public, the eternal and the contingent, the life and the work will inevitably collide and fuse. Lofty speculations must be shown to have arisen in time, in a sequence of other events, from the mind of a particular human being.
>
> The Transcendentalist practice suggests two characteristic and complementary American attitudes; an inclination to subordinate all activities to the recording of a life, and a reluctance to separate the work of art from the life of the artist, for fear, as Thoreau put it, "that the work of art should be at the expense of the man." In America all art tends towards the condition of autobiography, and all autobiography to the condition of life, but equally all life tends towards the condition of autobiography and all autobiography towards the condition of art. (Rosenwald 1988: 59).

The indissoluble link which Rosenwald sees between Transcendentalism, Americanness and self-representational writing indeed lends support to the hypothesis that online diaries are especially attuned to American social practises. Online diaries precisely merge public and private spaces in creative ways; online diaries also represent a way of turning oneself into the hero of one's own life, seen as a work of art and an ongoing creation. The philosophical trajectory charted by Emerson and encompassed in the concept of self-reliance finds direct expression in diaristic practices which attempt to construct a consistent though ever-evolving version of self through the painstaking analysis of the writer's inner life as well as through a description of the most mundane aspects of everyday life. The Transcendentalist search for the foundation of the new American self seeks precisely not to separate abstract thoughts from particulars; hence the entrenching of value into the miscellany of everyday life experience acquires all its meaning.

This stance is apparent in online diaries, which indeed often give the impression that what is recounted is tenuous, at several removes from any dramatic occurrence. The weather is often minutely described, and photographs of the sky or of clouds are provided. In Roland Barthes' analysis of diaristic small talk, the weather holds pride of place, in order "to tell the other that you are talking to him, to tell him nothing but this: I am talking to you, you exist for me, I want to exist for you. [...] Talking about the weather makes it possible for discourse to exist without saying anything. [...] Meaning only to tell the *nothingness* of my life (while avoiding its construction into a Destiny), the journal makes use of [...] the weather" (Barthes 1972: 174). The iterability of such notes, coupled with the endless changeability of the subject matter, combine to provide both writer and reader with a comfortable sense of dailiness that offers, as we shall see in a later chapter, a space for the self to grow and to reach out to others.

This is not to say that no serious or dramatic events ever find room in online diaries. Death and illness also get recorded, sometimes in poignant ways, as in *Dreaming Among the Jade Clouds*, where the suicide of the diarist was followed by one final entry written by her husband, after which the diary closed down. Sometimes historical events force their way into the diarists' world and become part of their interiority: this clearly happened for most of our sample after the September 11 attacks, or for some after the crash of TWA flight 700 to Paris.[7] The daily and the mundane predominate, however, because they are the most accessible parts of existence and can thus function as means to gain access to the very fabric of life.

2.2. Emerson and the ordinary

The necessary grounding of self-creation in the trivial may also be said to derive from another text, "The American Scholar," an address Emerson delivered to the Phi Beta Kappa Society at Cambridge in 1837, demonstrating how the convergence of self-reliance and the ordinary possesses definite repercussions for online diaries:

---

[7]   The Mighty Kymm, August 2, 1996 entry,
http://www.sweetasabiscuit.com/mightykymm/1996/august/080296.html

> Instead of the sublime and beautiful; the near, the low, the
> common, was explored and poetized. That, which had been
> negligently trodden under foot by those who were harnessing
> and provisioning themselves for long journeys into far
> countries, is suddenly found to be richer than all foreign parts.
> The literature of the poor, the feelings of the child, the
> philosophy of the street, the meaning of household life, are the
> topics of the time. It is a great stride. It is a sign, — is it not?
> of new vigor, when the extremities are made active, when
> currents of warm life run into the hands and the feet. I ask not
> for the great, the remote, the romantic; what is doing in Italy
> or Arabia; what is Greek art, or Provencal minstrelsy; I
> embrace the common, I explore and sit at the feet of the
> familiar, the low. Give me insight into to-day, and you may
> have the antique and future worlds. (Emerson 1849).

Emerson asserts that the familiar, the trivial, the commonplace are precisely what gives access to the essential reality of humanity, and his views are echoed with uncanny accuracy by the statement of intention of a diarists' webring: "No one's life is insignificant, no matter where they are, what they do, how old they are... Anyone's experiences can bring something to our lives – thought, perspective, laughs, tears".[8] Day after day, minute incidents get recorded, banal occurrences are deemed worthy of attention, small scale dramas are sometimes blown out of all proportion, moods and states of mind do not go unnoticed. Because the experiences of the small events of everyday life are widely shared, their investigation is required so that the reality common to all may emerge and lay the foundation for a new community. Because private events, no matter how outwardly insignificant, lay the groundwork for self-creation, they rightfully deserve the diarist's and the public's attention. Their availability to everyone turns them into evidence that domestic events are the stuff self-identity is made of, and that self-construction is attainable for every individual. The very dailiness of one's experience provides the basis for the construction of self and reasserts the democratic nature of Transcendentalist thinking.

2.3. Breaking with tradition

The stark contrast between European culture and day-to-day American experience also evidenced in this passage shows how

---

[8]   Open Pages, *op. cit.*, "Why a Webring ?", http://www.hedgehog.net/op/. Accessed December 2001.

Emerson attempts to sketch the outlines of a specifically American art grounded in the ordinary and the commonplace (Laugier 2002: 45). The construction of American culture rests on a break with and a redefinition of the European cultural heritage (Schirmeister 1999). This is not merely done to erase the past and shrug off the entire European literary tradition (Bloom 1984: 19-20).[9] Nor is it done to ignore the existing American tradition, but "by hook or by crook, to create room for a new one; as Bloom has shown, creating such space takes enormous leverage, whether for an individual or a nation, and to have leverage one must have a place to stand in. No text creates more space than does Emerson's 'American Scholar' " (Rosenwald 1988: 137). Emerson's personal declaration of independence from either moral or literary conformity is one that has resonated throughout American literature and philosophy, even though his own writing bespeaks the "permeating presence" (Weisbuch 1999: 204) of Old World culture.

In this context, the quest for self online diaries illustrate can be seen as an aspect of the wider American quest to ground value in the individual and to issue a declaration of independence from conformity and external rules – in other words, the American quest for self-reliance. Self-reliance should not, however, be mistaken for the assertion of a powerful 'I', but should be seen as referring to the construction of "a fragile self, pierced through and through by exteriority" (Laugier 2002: 53).[10] The search for self is but a way of exposing oneself to receiving a glimpse of pre-existing universals: "We lie in the lap of immense intelligence, which makes us receivers of its truth and organs of its activity. When we discern justice, when we discern truth we do nothing of ourselves, but allow a passage to its beams" (Emerson 1841). Emerson's insistence on the sheer fragility of the self and the fragility of its quest points to the fact that the search for value is, in and of itself, the end to strive for, rather than the setting up of norms which would but create a new kind of conformity. Thus does Emerson express his fundamental scepticism.

2.4. The quest for an American self

Interestingly, the Emersonian ideal of a break with the past to form the new American man was seminal to the thinking of another influential nineteenth century American thinker, Frederic J. Turner,

---

[9]   Quoted by Rosenwald, *op. cit.*, p. xi.
[10]   "La *self-reliance* n'est pas une constitution subjectivante, mais la constitution d'un soi fragile et pour ainsi dire traversé par l'extériorité".

whose 1893 frontier hypothesis also rested on the formation of a new American, unfettered by the constrictions of the past:

> From the conditions of frontier life came intellectual traits of profound importance. [...] That coarseness and strength combined with acuteness and inquisitiveness; that practical, inventive turn of mind [...] in spite of custom, each frontier did indeed furnish a new field of opportunity, a gate of escape from the bondage of the past; and freshness, and confidence, and scorn of older society, impatience of its restraints and ideas, and indifference to its lessons, have accompanied the frontier. (Turner 1921: 15-16)

This definition of Americanness is one that has left a lasting imprint on both academic and popular culture. William Boelhower has shown that this ideal American self had become ritualized in the early twentieth century by immigrants writing their autobiographies and attempting to conform to a dominant personal narrative of rebirth as a new individual in a new world:

> In fact, the specialty of ethnic autobiographical signification, its unique semiotic *jeu* largely consists in consciously re-elaborating or simply rewriting the received behavioral script of the rhetorically well-defined American self. [...] Like all initiation rites, the reading process began in the negative and required a stripping away of the 'old' self. [...] Due to xenophobic pressures [...] and the consequent need to allay spreading nativist fears, [...] most immigrant ethnic biographers sought to pass themselves off as Americans by didactically copying and promoting officially acceptable behavioural codes. (Boelhower 1991: 125-127).

Boelhower also identifies the literary *topoi* used in such texts and directly inspired by canonical American authors; success is viewed in Horatio-Algerean terms, "Whitmanian gaiety" regularly comes up to mark the emergence of a truly American self (Boelhower 1991: 129). "Part of the newness of American identity derives from the fact that it is supposedly self-made, self-determined, contractual and independent. Americans pride themselves on being a mobile, no-strings-attached, road people" (Boelhower 1991: 131).

The sub-genre of the ethnic diary appears online,[11] but the terms have changed since the nineteenth and early twentieth century. The

---

[11]   See for instance a webring for Asian journals, *The Rice Bowl Journals*, http://ricebowljournals.com or *Ayiah Net* /http://aiyah.net/index.htm or "Glass

essential point no longer resides in turning oneself into a seamless American, but in maintaining one's links with one's native country and reaching for multiculturalism. Aiyah for instance describes herself as "one and a half generation Chinese-American" and the title of her diary is "a very colloquial and common Chinese exclamation or phrase".[12] Despite knitting several scarves as Christmas gifts, she decorated her front door with a computer printout of mistletoe instead of using real leaves, writing she is "not crazy enough to drop money on stuff like this" and showing that her adoption of American social practises is not devoid of reservations.[13] In fact, cultural differentialism is used to ground her identity instead of being attenuated to the point of invisibility. Yet reading these journals quickly reveals that the link with the culture of origin is itself Americanized, so that Emerson's belief in the radical newness of American identity is still validated.

In addition, and because of the political dimension outlined in "American Scholar", the Emersonian concept of the ordinary refers to the relationship of an individual with the world at large. Emerson's search for relatedness to the world and to others thus provides a model for online diarists who reach out to others even while writing about the most private aspects of their lives because, like Emerson, they realize that they do not only construct themselves, but are continually constructed by others: "although Emerson declares that "man is the wonderworker" (*Collected Works* 1:89) and identifies his "one doctrine" as the infinitude of the private man" (*JMN* 7:342-43), these assertions are balanced (not contradicted) by his cautious and reverent attention to the subjectivity of the other" (Field 1997: 42).[14] Stressing the importance of relationships with others and with Nature as the primary Other refers to the basic incompletion of the isolated individual (Field 1997: 94). Desire for the Other as reader is precisely one of the reasons that seem to motivate online diarists.

Houses", a *Chicana* autobiography, http://www.cmp.ucr.edu/students/glasshouses . Accessed September 2001.
[12] http://aiyah.net/backbone.htm *op. cit.*
[13] *Ibid.*, December 25, 2003 entry.
http://www.aiyah.net/scribble/03/dec03/122503.htm
[14] Field's quotes refer to *The Collected Works of Ralph Waldo Emerson*, Robert Spiller *et al.* eds., Cambrige: Belknap Press of Harvard University Press, 1971; *The Journals and Miscellaneous Notebooks of Ralph Waldo Emerson, op. cit.*

3. Weblogs as dialogical spaces

In one of a collection of brief essays, Philippe Lejeune relates how he got the idea for the association for autobiography[15] he founded in 1992, after devoting most of his adult life to research on the same subject. Having launched a campaign to collect nineteenth century manuscript diaries, he frequently received responses from people who possessed no such document, but nevertheless offered their own diaries as research material. He comments on these offers as follows: "I admit this first made me smile, then dream. It took me some time to realize the huge *demand for a readership* which our society fails to meet" (Lejeune 1998: 49).[16]

This is precisely where Internet diaries and weblogs innovate most radically, in meeting this very demand. Not only do they make intimate writings potentially accessible to a multitude of readers, but they also make it possible to include the responses of the readers. In so doing, they set up a dense network of echoes and correspondences between diarist and audience and, more importantly still, they give it visibility.

Of course, earlier diaries were always written with an implicit reader in mind, as shown by the existence of revisions, drafts and final versions, as well as by the presence of intra-textual information about the "cast of characters" surrounding the writer. More fundamentally still, an implicit reader may be said to be immanent in any text, according to Wolfgang Iser:

> A text only becomes a reality if it is read in the conditions of actualisation that the text must bear within itself, hence the reconstruction of meaning by others. The idea of an implicit reader refers to a textual structure whereby the receiver is immanent. The receiver is a form that must be materialized, even if the text, through the fiction of a reader, does not seem to bother with an addressee, or even if it uses strategies aiming at excluding any possible public. The implicit reader is a conception which confronts the reader to the text in terms of

---

[15] Association pour l'autobiographie (APA), where anyone can deposit their diaries for safekeeping.

[16] "D'abord, je l'avoue, cela m'a fait sourire. Puis rêver. J'ai mis un certain temps à prendre conscience de l'immense *demande de lecture* à laquelle notre société n'offre aucune réponse". Emphasis in the text.

> textual effects, in relation to which understanding the text
> turns into an action. (Iser 1976: 70).[17]

If readers are structurally inscribed in any text, they do not, for all that, interact with it in any but a virtual fashion. No amount of notes or of study will ever modify the primary text which has set in motion the interpretative process. There can be no feedback or interaction between a printed text and its readership, unless another text is printed specifically for that purpose. Weblogs and journals modify this situation in depth. Whereas in traditional texts, the implicit reader is an effect contained within the text itself (Iser 1976: 76), online the readership is fleshed out. In online diaries, the responses are not virtual, but are emailed to the author, who may either keep them private or, in some cases, make them available alongside the text of the diary, as in Carolyn Burke's diary, or Terri's *Footnotes*. In addition, weblogs include software enabling readers' responses to be automatically posted and to appear next to the entry. Thus a dialogical space is created within what is supposed to be an intensely personal space.

3.1 Diaries as support systems

Reader responses are often greeted by an enthusiastic "yay!" or, in one instance, by the phrase "twenty-five people gave a damn",[18] expressing the diarist's joy at having been able to elicit one or more comments. One blogger, Aiyah, adopts the opposite attitude and writes 'two vomited" when signalling the existence of comments to an entry. Such a choice may either be ironic, or express the diarist's ambivalence towards her readers. More commonly, intense appreciation for readers' responses is a widespread phenomenon among diarists. Such enthusiasm points to the part played by the audience in offering various kinds of support to the diarist.

---

[17] "Le texte ne devient une réalité que s'il est lu dans des conditions d'actualisation que le texte doit porter en lui-même, d'où la reconstruction du sens par autrui. L'idée d'un lecteur implicite se réfère à une structure textuelle d'immanence du récepteur. Il s'agit d'une forme qui doit être matérialisée, même si le texte, par la fiction du lecteur, ne semble pas se soucier de son destinataire, où même s'il applique des stratégies qui visent à exclure tout public possible. Le lecteur implicite est une conception qui situe le lecteur face au texte en termes d'effets textuels par rapport auxquels la compréhension devient un acte".
[18] *Dirty Feet and Lily-White Intentions, op. cit.*

3.1.1. Psychological support

Most online diaries or blogs contain an 'about' section, in which a self-description is provided. The profile itself is often, though not always, dictated by a template provided by the online journal software and subsequently fleshed out by the whole diary. These self-descriptions, formatted as they are by the software, nevertheless hark back to well-established models of self-representational writing. Cardano or Montaigne in the sixteenth century, for instance, described their physical and moral characteristics, and more particularly their flaws, with apparently uncompromising openness. Closer to us, Emerson wrote with poignancy in his *Journals* about what he perceived to be his inadequacies:

> There exists a signal defect of character which neutralizes in great part the just influence my talents ought to have. […] Its bitter fruits are a sore uneasiness in the company of most men & women, a frigid fear of offending & jealousy of disrespect, an inability to lead & an unwillingness to follow the current conversation, which contrive to make me second with all those among whom chiefly I wish to be first. […] I am unfortunate also […] in a propensity to laugh or rather snicker. I am ill at ease therefore among men. […] A score of words and deeds issue from me daily, of which I am not the master. […] In my frequent humiliation, even before women & children I am compelled to remember the poor boy who cried, "I told you, Father, they would find me out" (Porte, Morris, 2001: 486-487).

This self-assessment is especially striking as it illustrates how, in trying to set down for the benefit of others the kind of person he is, Emerson cannot help but perceive the *unheimlich* within himself. When he ruefully mentions the uncontrolled words and laughter that escape him, Emerson realizes that something he cannot either identify or acknowledge is trying to emerge and to be disclosed. Failing to master his own words or laughter, losing face because of his absence of self-control, Emerson seems to become aware of his own symbolic castration, which reveals to him his own finiteness; he even loses any solid grounding for his identity; his fear of being found out indicates a deep-seated doubt about himself and about the congruence of his inner self with his public image. He fears he might be an impostor whose real nature can be seen through. This is one of the reasons why he needs to use his writing on the blank page as he would use his reflection in a mirror, in order to re-establish his vacillating sense of self. Then the narration of his progress may be read and responded to by a reader whose identification with the writer might induce the same kind of questioning.

A similar exposition of physical or psychological flaws is a recurrent feature in the self-descriptions provided by diarists, with, however, a wide variety of effects, as can be seen in the following example:

> I'm Beth, I'm 34. I am a criminal defense attorney in Sacramento, California. I do appeals, which means I sit in an office and write things and never wear a suit. Except when I have oral argument, which I almost never do. In 2003 I won a major case in the California Supreme Court, and I am telling you about it because the odds are it will never happen again. For the past two years I have also been working on an M.A. in English, because I am certifiably insane. My Supreme Court oral argument happened the week after my spring finals, which should help you evaluate the current level of my insanity.[19]

In this case the flaws are so overstated that they verge on the hyperbolic. The effect is therefore humorous, exaggeration undercutting the apparent negative meaning of the words used. However, both this diarist's and Emerson's self-descriptions represent a model readers may respond to dialogically: the way the writers relate to their own perceived strangeness may get readers thinking about their own inner processes and set in motion an exchange of correspondence that may also help assuage some of the self-loathing apparent in these passages.

3.1.2. Recognition

Another purpose of the initial self-portrait in online diaries is seduction: appealing to a large number of readers and having them respond, meets a deep-seated need for love and recognition. The seductive strategies rely on a careful mix of self-revelation and coyness. The example provided by Kevin's diary, *Change Over Time,* is quite characteristic. First he entitles the section "This Strange, Eventful History", thus immediately evoking intertextuality, since this is a quotation from Shakespeare's *As You like It,* more precisely the end of the "All the world's a stage" speech. Such a title raises a set of expectations in readers, the least of which is not the allusion to

---

[19] Beth's *Bad Hair Days,* http://www.xeney.com/about.html . Accessed January 2002.

theatricality and masks, and hence to a mystery encouraging them to read on. The first line, "I'm thirty-two years old, gay and male," is simple and introduces a complex narrative taken up with purely professional dilemmas, since the writer has had to give up a doctoral program at Harvard to become a junior-high school teacher. But the narrative is interspersed with subtitles and notations hinting at more personal content, links are provided to entries that are important to the writer, and it is only at the very end that his "coming-out story" appears, in no less than two instalments.[20] This diarist ends with thanks to his readers, thus giving full expression to the recognition he seeks.

Recognition may be defined as the reaction from the other which lends meaning to one's actions or emotions, thus enabling the self to develop to the full. Recognition, in other words, is a necessary condition for an inter-subjective relationship. This is indeed what seems to occur when a reader comments on an entry: the diarist may feel validated by having been relevant or funny enough to have encouraged someone to click on the message link; conversely, readers get an additional incentive to keep on responding when seeing the enthusiastic reception they have elicited, and the reciprocal relationship is an incentive to keep on interacting. Each diarist thus creates a small web of connections, where relationships may become just as intense as they may be offline.

3.1.3. Social Support

Personal storytelling involves sustained efforts to recover the substance of past events or to give accurate expression to the feelings or states of mind of the diarist. This task is by definition one that diarists must accomplish on their own, as they are the only repositories of their memories – and of the lapses of memory which are just as constitutive of a subject as what is remembered. Indeed, diaristic narratives are delimited both by what is said and by what diarists cannot say, illustrating Lacan's concept that the subject is constituted around an originary lack. This lack is precisely what impels various forms of personal storytelling. The blanks in diaristic narratives do not make them any less truthful, but may provide the space necessary for diarists to write and for readers to respond.

Indeed, the very difficulty of remembering and ordering personal narratives suggests that the presence of others is not a mere chance,

---

[20]   http://kevin.diary-x.com/?entry=bio

but a genuine requirement if the effort is to be sustained. Sharing one's inner life and one's life story with others is a way of inviting society to bear witness to the discovery of one's historicity, one's position in time, one's progression from earlier versions of oneself to the time of writing. Because the consciousness of oneself as a subject can never be a given, these private writings are permeated with the concern with readers, who provide the mirror from which it will become possible to talk about oneself. This is apparent in Miles Hochsteins' *Documented Life*: not only does the writer encourage readers to email him, but he also offers them a space on his own site to post their pictures or life stories, which he refers to by the word 'mirror', suggesting both a 'mirror site', i.e. a website reproducing the content of a given page on a different server, and a looking glass. Specularity thus appears at the very heart of self-representational writing.

Lacan's concept of the mirror stage rests on the idea that either a looking glass or a person serving as a substitute for one gives the infant a chance to perceive her body as a whole, thus making her first steps on the road to selfhood and, by perceiving a symmetrical image of herself, gaining a sense of her own otherness. The function of the mirror is to provide a medium for the identification to others as well as for separation from others. When Miles encourages others to put up their own material within his own Internet space, he is inviting others to act as a mirror to himself; when writing about himself, he is offering himself up as a mirror to others. The whole process aims at allowing participants to constitute one another as subjects. When asking others to contact him, Miles is calling on them to identify and respond to the originary lack around which he is constituted. In Miles' own words, email "completes the communication loop": the word 'loop', indicating as it does a system operating on the basis of feedback, also points to the community formation that may be said to underlie much of online diaristic writing.

3.2. Community building

Difficulty in meeting other people and connecting to them is indeed one of the best researched aspects of contemporary social relationships. The reasons invoked for this situation may vary widely, as do the strategies devised by individuals to remedy this situation. The following excerpt from Columbine's journal illustrates the way in which online communities reproduce the cleavages, and hence the isolation, of offline ones:

> Rose [the diarist's wife] thinks she has the answer. She's been
> trying to hook me up with an alleged peer group for ages.
> However, I refuse to believe they're my peer group. Actually,
> that's not quite true; they're probably my peer group, but I
> refuse to believe that they would be able to provide me the
> conversational relief that I desire, because they're all
> intimidatingly smart - a hell of a lot smarter and faster on their
> feet than I am - and I know from experience how much trouble
> I have talking to some of them. [...] I'm thinking of starting
> my own group. I will call it The Reasonably Brilliant
> Underachievers. We'll get together and be confident enough
> that we each have moderately passable intelligence and
> knowledge that we will have no need to flaunt it or even make
> it visible in any obvious way. [...] We will all be comfortable
> in one another's presence, and we will therefore be free to talk
> intelligently about books we love and movies we hate and
> home repair and sex and history and the state of the world and
> each others' lives. And we will be friends. And we will care
> about what happens to each other.[21]

What the above quote illustrates is a social utopia rid of any drive
towards domination and power, such as may be founded by online
diarists. It also foregrounds the need to mix the trivial small talk of
daily life with more abstract conversation and emotional involvement.
This passage with its half-nostalgic, half-ironic yearning for
friendship, might almost be characterized as an apt description of
interactions in blogs and online diaries. Such interactions may be said
to function as hubs towards the formation of micro-communities
based on elective affinities and sometimes, though not necessarily, on
geographical proximity. By seductively opening up their lives for
scrutiny, one of the expectations of diarists is not only meeting other
people, but enlisting their active cooperation in the creation of an
inner circle, a small group of people gathered around certain
characteristics—in the above example, a rivalry-free, ideal community
of equals.

Such groups keep being formed, both online and offline. Terri
created a society all of whose members met through their online
diaries.[22] The other two major members, Bitter Hag and Bev Sykes, all
live in Terri's vicinity and share her newfound passion for bicycle
riding, demonstrating in this case the overlap of proximity and

---

[21]   Alewife Bayou, http://www.eccentricflower.com/pihua/200312/entry4.htm,
December 20, 2003.
[22]   The society is called 'Boobs', an acronym standing for 'Babes on Outrageous
Bicycles'.

community.[23] One of them volunteered to type up all the old journals written by Terri in the seventies so that they could be uploaded on the Internet. The readers thus not only turn into actors in the diaristic narrative of one individual, but also actually take part in the formation of the diary itself.

Another diarist, Shmuel, undertook a long bus tour from New-York to Boston to Canada and then to Texas and back, for the purpose of meeting some of his numerous readers. His trip then appeared in a number of entries of his own blog, complete with links to the corresponding entries in the diaries of his correspondents. The network of echoes resonating from one diary to the next can be even more complex. For instance, one of Shmuel's friends whom he symbolically calls his "sister", Erin, visited him at Ann Arbor. She documented this on her site, providing a photograph to which Shmuel linked in turn in his own December 30, 2002 entry.[24] Similarly, Shmuel paid a visit to Mary Anne, who uploaded a few photographs of him on her own site, which Shmuel again linked to.[25] With these pictures and comments, and the dense interlinking between several diaries, therefore, his correspondents simultaneously contribute to building up his diary and gain a foothold in its writing space. They also act in a similar fashion when they send him comical identity quizzes to answer, with questions such as "Which Greek goddess are you ?" or "What muppet are you ?"[26], or "What irrational number are you ?" which all appear on Shmuel's blog.[27]   Free association exercises entitled "Unconscious Mutterings"[28] often simultaneously sprout up in the respective journals of a group of friends, and these sometimes constitute the only text in a daily entry, a way of minimally keeping in touch with friends and readers. More basically, Shmuel often announces public events such as poetry readings, asking

---

[23]   Bitter Hag, http://www.bitterhag.com/index.asp; Bev Sykes' diary, *Funny the World*, http://www.funnytheworld.com/ . Accessed November 2002.
[24]   Erin's *Well Notes*, December 30, 2002 entry,
http://wellnotes.treacle.net/archives/travelling.shtml
[25]   Mary Anne's Journal, June 24, 2002 entry,
http://www.mamohanraj.com/journal/show-entry.php?Entry_ID=428 , linked by Shmuel on December 29, 2002.
[26]   February 27, 2002 entry,
http://www.babeltower.org/soapbox/blog/2002_02_24_old.html
[27]   November 4, 2003 entry,
http://www.babeltower.org/soapbox/blog/2003_11_02_old.html
[28]   See for instance the August 31, 2003 entry,
http://www.babeltower.org/soapbox/blog/2003_08_31_old.html or the entry dated October 19, 2003, http://www.babeltower.org/soapbox/blog/2003_10_19_old.html

interested people to "drop [him] a line".[29] This request is significant, for the announcement could have been made in the entry without further ado. Asking readers to write is a way of asking them to express a symbolic desire for the writer. Shmuel himself comments on the link between self-chronicling and socializing early on:

> You know, people say the Internet makes people anti-social, keeps them from having a life... I wouldn't have a social life at *all* if not for the 'Net!
>
> This is all true, you know. It's also one reason why I'm reluctant to leave New York. Almost everyone comes to New York eventually, so I'm *able* to meet net.friends [sic] every now and then. Somehow, I can't imagine this happening nearly as often in Michigan.[30]

Online diaries thus repeatedly provide illustrations of their socializing functions, as hypertextual links with other people's diaries turn into real life interconnections.

A final example illustrates how far this search for the Other can go. A diarist called Rachel created a specific rubric within her own diary in order to keep a trace of the numerous web pages created by another weblogger, Catherine.[31] She then proceeded to give a full account of the way in which their friendship evolved and of the projects they shared, giving links to all the entries where Catherine is mentioned, as well as links to the latter's former web pages. In this case, interlinking gives way to the actual merging of two diaries. Similarly, some of the pages written by Bev Sykes upon the death of two of her children are reproduced in one of her friends' site. She writes: "My friend Steve Schalchlin read something I wrote on a forum recently and designed a web page for me. I was touched that he'd think it good enough to work with".[32] Networking with other diarists can therefore be said to loom large in the expectations of diarists, and may actually end up in a process of co-enunciation. Whenever diarists reserve part of their site to others, they are taking steps, however tentatively, towards the formation of a stable community.

---

[29]   April 27, 2001 entry,
http://www.babeltower.org/soapbox/blog/2001_04_22_old.html
[30]   March 18, 2001 entry,
http://www.babeltower.org/soapbox/blog/2001_03_18_old.html
[31]   Rachel's Daily Diary, http://www.reinyday.com/rachel/daily/entry/catherine.html
[32]   http://wheel.dcn.davis.ca.us/~basykes/homepage.html

The 'contact' or 'notify' list also points to an effort at community building. In this way, diarists are trying to identify their readers and to get to know more about them. Sometimes they try to entice readers to 'get notified' by pointing out that such readers are allowed to receive more detailed or more intimate entries. Thus, Shmuel wrote when he began dating, that people on his 'notify list' got to hear "a bit more", albeit "not terribly much".[33] Shmuel pushes the logic a step further when he offers his readers a quiz about himself, entitled "How well do you know me?" and then publishes the results.[34] His analysis of the twenty-four responses shows him to be puzzling as to who his readers might be, especially those among them who displayed uncanny knowledge of his life while being completely unknown to him.

In a more far-reaching development of the same idea, a webring, Live Journal, will allow new members to join only if they are given a password by someone who is already a member, thus carrying over in online environments the age-old notion of sponsoring. This bid to identify writers of diaries and readers aims at creating an inner circle that will be privy to personal information and become more closely-knit as a result. The public weblog or journal thus spawns a more private version set apart for the self-selected few willing to relinquish their position of silent lurkers to interact with the diarist and lay the foundations for the emergence of a community.

3.3. Polyphony

The inclusion of readers' comments, their actual participation in building up the text of the diary, the inclusion of heterogeneous texts sent by correspondents: these features conform with Mikhail Bakhtine's concept of polyphony which identifies the co-presence of multiple, often contradictory discourses within the same text, without any possibility of these discourses being unified by a single subjectivity, be it that of the author or in the present case, of the diarist (Bakhtine 1970: 46-48). Because of the dialogical space produced by the interactions between writer and readers, the self produced through the diaristic narrative is unambiguously a multiple one, in which the private dimensions intertwine with the social dimensions, akin to what Lejeune defined as "networked intimacy" (Lejeune 2000b: 227). The multiplicity of the self that emerges in traditional and online diaries is

---

[33] August 6, 2003 entry,
http://www.babeltower.org/soapbox/blog/2003_08_03_old.html
[34] February 8, 2002 entry,
http://www.babeltower.org/soapbox/blog/2002_02_03_old.html

also due to the nature of language which, because of its structure, is necessarily polysemous. Therefore, writing about the self "sets up a polyphonic enunciation [...] that is at the same time limited and validated by the desire for a discourse which will elicit a response" (Harel 1997: 169).[35]

Still, we have to remember that the additions provided by others are subordinated to and incorporated into the text written by the diarist, whose voice remains the main center of the self-representational text. Because of this hierarchical relationship, weblogs transform the usual back-and-forth movement of a face-to-face conversation, where one must give way to others and remain silent for a while if one is to enter into interaction with others (Flahault 1999: 71). The voice of the diarist essentially controls the dialogical space.

This point being granted, we have to acknowledge that such inclusions initiate a process of reciprocity that is the essence of desire. Pleas for contact are found on each and every site. Writing an online personal narrative is a way of seductively reaching out to others by expressing the lack that founds any desire. Posting online comments means responding to that desire, giving oneself permission to interact playfully or seriously with others, unveiling the truth of the diarist and in the process unveiling one's own truth. Diaristic narratives dramatize the fact that the relationship to self-chronicling, just like the relationship to the fictional construct of self, is in fact built around an open-endedness which is the mark of desire. The online dialogical space set up by the responses to diary entries dramatizes the relationship of reciprocal desire, built around language, between diarists and their audience. Being touched by and responding to an entry means willingly accepting to be seduced, willingly suspending disbelief in the non-importance of such interactions. This is akin to what Lacan referred to in one of his most famous puns, by "les non-dupes errent" (Lacan 1973b):[36] reading a text and relating to the writer, joining the fray of mutual desire, willingly being duped, and embracing the mutual illusion of *rapport*. "There is no such thing as sexual intercourse", also wrote Lacan famously (Lacan 1973a: 11).[37]

---

[35] "L'écriture du récit de soi instaure une polyphonie énonciative [...], parole à la fois contrainte et validée par ce souhait d'une parole qui trouve un répondant".

[36] The title of the seminar is a pun on "les noms du père" (the names of the father), and "non-dupes are wrong". The transcription of the seminar is available online, http://perso.wanadoo.fr/espace.freud/topos/psycha/psysem/nondup/nondup1.htm

[37] "Il n'y a pas de rapport sexuel"

By the same token, "there is no such thing as textual intercourse" – but what does exist is desire for the Other, the Other as body, and the Other as text. The psychological space thus cleared out is precisely what makes space for sociability both online and offline.

4. Conversation societies

If the explicit presence of a readership can lead diarists to meet their readers in real life, it may also result in another interesting development, in that the conversation may take place not merely with the diarist herself, but between readers of a diary. As explained by Mary Anne, one of the earliest online diarists, in a conversation with Jed, her partner in real life, but also a fellow writer and online blogger, comments systems have deeply modified the function of diaries:

> *Mary-Ann*: In December of 1995, I started my own online journal on my web page. I've been updating it more and more frequently ever since. At the beginning, it was probably only a few entries a month; now it's gotten to the point of several a day. And just last month, I added a comments system [...], so that the community of readers who have grown up around my journal can talk directly to each other, instead of just sending e-mail to me.
>
> *Jed*: And though I was slow to get on the bandwagon, I've come to see comments systems as an important part of community-building. Writers with journals could always post comments to each other in their own journals, but a journal with a comments system built in allows for brief, informal, and frequent comments. It also links a community together: you don't have to go searching for other journals of like-minded people, you can just follow links to the home pages and journals of people who comment on your journal, and the links grow. (Mohanraj, Hartmann 2003).

Two important ideas appear in this passage: one of them is that the communities built around a single writer end up developing almost autonomously when room is made for their participation. The second idea is that readers are looking for people they can relate to and identify with, not for original lives or penetrating comments. Familiarity and informality are key to the development of a large body of texts contributed by diary readers.

However, these reader responses deeply modify our interpretation of the primary text, i.e. the diarist's text. The author is no longer unique, the classical writing space is no longer one person's alone, but is shared by a collective. Diarists then become at the same time the observed and the observer: they become the observers of their own lives and play the part of the observed for whoever interacts with them. What used to be a soliloquy turns into more than a dialogue – a multilogue. In Mary Anne's words, "It's a big step, to open up a comments section, to allow the readers to talk to each other. I find it a little scary, to be honest" (Mohanraj, Hartmann 2003). The loss of control over one's private web space, however limited it might be, can indeed be unsettling if it forces the diarist into a re-evaluation of her relationship with her audience.

Such a reader-to-reader relationship appears in Greg's diary where, after asking his readers to consult his Amazon wish list and to post theirs, no less than thirty-eight responses were posted.[38] Sixteen different readers contributed one or more responses either to Greg or to each other, while the diarist himself only wrote six of them. The group interacting around Greg seems to be bound by close ties, with members who are familiar to one another and who join the conversation in an easy, informal way.

The observation of Mary Anne's weblog, on the other hand, does not support the hypothesis of an autonomous discussion among readers, without reference to the diarist. All the responses address questions asked by the diarist or issues raised by her, so that the conversation still centers around her. This is apparent in the following example, after Mary Anne wondered whether printing a newsletter and sending it to her acquaintances for Christmas would be "tacky" or boastful.[39] The various comments elicited by her request show her to be the primary interlocutor:

> *David Bellamy*: Come on, Mary Anne! You are entitled to brag !
>
> *Mary Anne*: Oh, it's not that, exactly. I'm just not sure if Christmas cards are the appropriate place for it... feels a bit weird.
>
> *Dayle*: When I receive a commercial card that just has a signature in it, I wonder, why bother? I do appreciate people thinking of me, but I'd MUCH rather get a newsy letter, or even a picture, instead of this impersonal waste of a tree.
>
> *Karen*: I'm a big fan of holiday cards. When I was younger I took them for granted, but as time goes by and my friends are

---

[38] Greg Van Eekhout, *The Official Voice of the American People*, December 4, 2003. http://www.journalscape.com/greg/

[39] Mary Anne's *Ongoing, Erratic Journal, op. cit.*, December 6, 2003, http://www.mamohanraj.com/journal/show-entry.php?Entry_ID=1594

> spread far and wide in the world, this is one time of year when it's wonderful to feel their continuing presence in my life. When I open a card from a good friend and see nothing but a signature I do think it's a little lame, but […] I'm not looking a gift card in the mouth.
>
> Printed-out letters are not tacky if they're written with flair and good humor, and addressed openly to everyone (rather than striking the blatantly false pose of speaking to an individual recipient). Think of it as a journal entry in which you're summing up the year, and it'll be a pleasure to receive.
>
> *Mary Anne*: I'm over it -- the letters are written and going in. With photos, even. And poetry.:-)

The above example clearly shows that interaction takes place between diarist and reader rather than between readers themselves. Each contribution is a discrete unit, leaving no unfinished sentence to be completed by others, for instance, as often happens in instant messaging systems. Even if the responses span a short period of time, as in the above example, where less than two hours separate the original question from its final resolution, asynchronicity predominates, giving participants time to write out careful sentences. As a result, the conversation is one-to-many and vice-versa, rather than many-to-many.

This does not detract from the importance of the discursive activity in weblogs, because the responses contribute to elaborating on the meaning of the 'primary text' that the entry constitutes. As such, they function in a manner similar to the back and forth movement between speakers in one-to-one conversational interactions, where each participant expects the other to take their words into account, with the important difference that here, Mary Anne is carrying out a one-to-one conversation with several people simultaneously. But the disciplined turn-taking fashion in which exchanges are organized means that there is none of the tentativeness or indecisiveness characteristic of face-to-face interactions.

This written-out conversation also modifies the position of the reader who is invited to step into that space. The frontier between writer and readers is no longer impassable, diarists relinquish some of their centrality, and readers are in fact expected to contribute to structuring the text of the blog by participating in the collective writing of entries, thus imprinting their mark on the diary. This literally happens in a weblog where readers are invited to contribute

ideas to a story, which then appears online as a collective text.[40]
Readers thus produce the text, while the text produces them as both
readers and writers. Diarists encourage this collaborative process
which deprives them of their own space, as if in recognition of the fact
that the narrative of self cannot emerge in isolation. The private
domain is totally open to the world-at-large, seemingly blurring the
inside/outside divide through the constant intrusions of others in that
private space.

4.1. Conversational mode

Weblogs and diaries differ in the way the responses of readers are
organized. The diaristic form keeps up the familiar patterns of
traditional correspondence, where letters were expected to be shared
by several members of the same family or of the same circle of
friends. Traditional online diaries may or may not include the emails
received by the writer. If they do appear, they may be carefully edited
to display only a few significant excerpts, for instance. Email may
remain completely private, and only appear as a short reference within
the text of an entry. The diarist therefore remains completely in
control of what does or does not appear on a page.

Weblogs are different inasmuch as the software is in charge of
displaying readers' answers; the blogger has very little scope for
editing or deleting answers. In addition, responding to an entry is
usually not done through email but through a form located at the
bottom of the page. The very great ease with which such forms can be
uploaded leads readers to use a conversational mode which I proposed
to call a quasi-oral genre in the context of newsgroups (Serfaty 2002b:
187), and which I propose to refer to as 'oralized writing' in the
blogging context. The distinction between the kind of language used
on blogs and newsgroups appears to be an important one. Messages in
newsgroups attempt to make up for the dryness of the text-only
environment by using a variety of strategies reintroducing the rhythms
of speech of face-to-face conversation. In instant messaging systems,
the goal is the same, but the inbuilt technical constraints lead to the
use of a large number of abbreviations that sometimes need to be read
aloud in order to be understood. Blogs do not come up against the
same difficulty, firstly because they are asynchronous, and secondly
because they enable the use of pictures and sounds, thus supplying a

---

[40] *Dirty Feet and Lily White Intentions, op. cit.*, December 22, 2003,
http://lilywhiteintentions.com/

more densely contextualized discourse. Webloggers nevertheless tend to preserve an appearance of spontaneity through a variety of strategies, whose general drift is to reproduce the immediacy of exchanges where participants are co-present.

In responses to weblog entries, we may note a tendency towards very short sentences, sometimes isolated words, that are very close to phatic utterances, those sounds which, according to Roman Jakobson, maintain contact with the speaker and are meant to indicate that the audience is listening and interested in what is being said. Another feature of blogging responses is the use of punctuation in erratic ways meant to make it more expressive, with the over-use of three dots as a way of indicating indeterminacy, either pauses or the hesitations characteristic of face-to-face conversations. The brevity of a response to any given entry indicates its kinship with a micro-text attempting to mime orality. This is confirmed by the repetitions of a few words taken from the entry, as often happens in face-to-face conversations. Moreover, the general tone of such responses is that of compliments or praise, sometimes stopping just this side of flattery. Compliments being traditionally interpreted as verbal gifts (Wauthion 2000: 15), the emphasis on praise can be perceived as a way of facilitating exchanges and interaction through the twin action of aggrandizing the diarist, while minimizing one's achievements. Exaggeration is the rule in such compliments (Bays 2000: 177). This is apparent in the following example, after a description by the diarist of the scarves she is knitting:

> 1) you are soooooo good at knitting! very impressive! hope you're having happy holidays!:) (Dec 14, 2003 - gg)
>
> 2) u have a great talent for knitting.make me jealous.:D n you did lots and good products (December 15, 2003- Kiki)
>
> 3) I'm absolutely useless at knitting. I remember my grandma trying to teach me… I wasn't a very good student, sad to say:) Very nice creations you've made and just in time for the holidays! Happy holidays ! (December 15, 2003 – Sinta).[41]

The hyperbolic compliments are paralleled by equally overstated self-disparagement, in which the speaker allows herself to be seen as lacking, the better to state her allegiance to the diarist, who remains the central figure in this micro-community.

---

[41] *Aiyah's Net, op. cit.*, http://www.aiyah.net/blogger.html . Accessed December 2003.

4.2. The oralization of writing

In addition to the generally laudatory tone of these comments, we can also note a playful kind of spelling typically relying on vowel repetition, as a way of imitating the lexical stress or the sentence stress of English. According to Serge Tisseron, the keyboard is actually conducive to disregard of the rules of proper spelling because it frees us from the rigors of our early training. When writing with pen on paper, we are bound by all the rules we were taught as children and which we have internalised. The keyboard, on the other hand, is often a self-taught skill and is free of any painful associations with red ink, low grades or punishments. Writing with the help of a keyboard may thus release the writer from the fear of the schoolteacher, who to the child is possessed with knowledge and legitimacy (Tisseron 2001: 65-69). An additional reason why people rarely correct their spelling mistakes when responding to an entry is that they are attempting to preserve the appearance of spontaneous speech and of immediacy, with their attendant disregard for the conventions of proper spelling. Another feature of oralized writing is the elision of some personal pronouns, compounding the effects of spontaneity and naturalness sought in the comments sections of weblogs.

The oralization of writing may actually take the form of stage directions, as can be seen in the following attempt at reproducing actual speech as well as describing actions and emotions:

> And please tell me that you're making up the Narnia bit. *Please. [Googles it]*
> Oh, God. You're not. Aiiiiiiieeeeeee!
> *[reads more closely]* Oh, just the digital effects. Not the script adaptation or anything else.
> *[Heart rate returns to normal. Or as normal as it can get while still being faced with the dismal spectre of anybody trying to make a major motion picture out of Narnia. Wasn't the BBC version good enough?]* Sorry about that... carry on.[42]

The use of the conventions of stage directions gives verbal form to what the technological set-up of computer-mediated communication conceals behind the double veils of the screen and of the written word, i.e. the bodily actions expressing the emotions of the speaker. They

---

[42]   Mary Anne Mohanraj, *An Ongoing, Erratic Journal, op. cit.* Shmuel, one of the diarists being studied here, (http://www.babeltower.org/soapbox/blog/) is commenting on the entry dated December 18, 2003, 10:31 a.m., http://www.mamohanraj.com/journal/index.php . Italics added.

point at a self-conscious use of language akin to a meta-discourse creating a micro-context for the informal remarks constituting the body of the message. Accordingly, the stage directions take up more space than Shmuel's remarks themselves, which remain colloquial and informal. The general effect is not so much theatrical as humorous, because it relies on the use of hyperbole, a trope which turns out to be in heavy use in such contexts, as an antidote to the austerity of text. An added bonus in this kind of oralization is the strong suggestion of dialogue it evokes, as can be seen with the use of conversational interjections ('Oh, God', 'oh', 'please', 'carry on' etc.).

Unlike the above example, however, the brevity of most responses does not leave much scope to content, but underscores their closeness with conversation and hence with social activity. Conversation is often the art of sweet or not-so-sweet nothings, sometimes actually empty of meaning, but whose ultimate purpose still is of considerable importance. The merest phatic utterance, such as 'oh', maintains the channels of communication open, contributes to support the diarist in his drive towards personal storytelling as well as sustaining social communication through the reproduction of traditional modes of sociability. The dialogues initiated by weblogs may be only marginally significant as far as their internal meaning is concerned, but they nevertheless function as markers of the acknowledgement of other subjectivities. They institute an I-Thou relationship, because even one who talks about nothing is still attempting to reach out to another individual. The language used in responses to weblog entries, through the oralization of writing, attempts a reproduction of the casual conversations of everyday life which underpin one's sense of existence as a social being. The concatenation of juxtaposed responses to an entry provides the warp and woof for the fabric of the micro-society created by a weblog and its audience.

Chapter Three

Humor in Cyberspace

Online diaries conform to the general tendency of websites towards playfulness, no matter how serious their purpose might be (Serfaty 2002a: 81). Humor being in and of itself a playful manipulation of language, its prevalence in Internet self-representational writings comes as no surprise. In the flood of diaristic narratives found on the Internet, humor is indeed used under various guises. The definition of humor, however, is notoriously elusive (Evrard 1996: 3). Relying as it does on an indissociable mix of form and content, and making use of the twin tropes of condensation and displacement to enable latent meanings to become manifest (Evrard 1996: 107), its success depends on knowledge and assumptions shared by the audience. Humor is therefore both historically and socially determined, and attempting an essentializing definition may prove to be arduous, if not downright impossible. Rather than seeking such a definition, then, I propose to take a look at the techniques used in humor, before investigating its functions in the framework of online diaristic writing.

1. Juxtaposition

Humor may arise from the juxtaposition of disparate categories; the slight skewing produced by such disparity calls attention to itself, thwarts conventional expectations and exposes the seamy underbelly of reality that decorousness usually manages to keep covered up. By warping language ever so slightly, humor therefore points to the existence of a chasm yawning underneath ordinary words. In weblogs, where oralized writing subtly mixes the features of the spoken and the written word, humor derives on the one hand from the incongruous juxtaposition of words and on the other hand from the juxtaposition of media. As I pointed out early on, most online diaries use text as well as drawings, photographs and sometimes audio recordings of the diarist's own voice. The juxtaposition of different media is used for humorous effect through a process of either illustration or counterpoint. In the following example, one of the photos provided is that of a grimacing young woman's face, while another one shows the diarist with her tongue sticking out.[1] The entry reads as follows:

> In the first pictures taken of me as a newborn, I look like an oversized, partially digested tadpole with a bad case of sunburn and a toaster for a head; my parents hold me in their laps and stare down at me with frozen smiles of dismay while my grandmother leafs through the baby book looking for a name that means "lumpen blob" in Welsh. Matters did not improve much in my early childhood; in my Sears baby portraits, I worked the giant-muffin-with-arms look, and then my parents, apparently in an effort to snag the prize money in some sort of Scariest Two-Year-Old In New Jersey contest, took a series of photos of me in all my just-bathed, stark-naked, Gorgon-headed toddler glory[2].

On the surface, the hyperbolic description of ugliness, which comes complete with mythological references to the Gorgon, is meant to reinforce the significance of the supposedly ugly photograph illustrating it. The snapshots act as a sort of visual match for the text. In addition, the similes all tend to liken the newborn baby to either an animal ('tadpole') or a thing ('toaster, blob, giant muffin'), a metamorphosis which casts off the baby into the realm of the non human (Evrard 1996: 119). On a deeper level, however, exaggeration is a time-honored, humor-creating rhetorical device aimed at undermining and even reversing the ostensible meaning of the text and of the pictures interwoven with it. The snapshots of the supposedly unprepossessing young woman mesh with the hyperbolically exaggerated description of ugliness to produce the exact opposite of dismay or horror – laughter and admiration for the wit of the writer.

---

[1]   "Picture Imperfect: So Many Chins, So Little Time".
http://www.tomatonation.com/picture2.asp. Accessed January 2003.
[2]   "Picture Imperfect: Don't Point that Thing at Me".
http://www.tomatonation.com/picture.asp. Accessed January 2003. This entry and all subsequent quotations from diaries are unedited.

On the other hand, next to the picture of Terri, a pretty smiling brunette, the text reads: "First the bad news: I am a cranky, self-absorbed, fortysomething/ noncustodial mom/ recovering alcoholic/ newlywed/ transplanted-Seattleite-turned-California-Girl... and I write about it in relentless, mind-numbing detail on the Internet every day".[3] The "good news" is, predictably in the humorous context, absolutely identical. Here, text and image clash and thus heighten the comic effect through counterpoint and the tension between visual and lexical elements it affords. This kind of 'incongruity' was seen by Arthur Schopenhauer to be essential to eliciting laughter:

> The origin of the ludicrous is always the paradoxical, and thus unexpected, subsumption of an object under a concept that is in other respects heterogeneous to it. Accordingly, the phenomenon of laughter always signifies the sudden apprehension of an incongruity between such a concept and the real object thought through it, and hence between what is abstract and what is perceptive. (Schopenhauer 1969: 91)

Some diarists base their humor primarily on text: thus Shmuel uses the lyrics of a song as an epigraph and wry commentary on his entry about the choice of Joe Lieberman as Al Gore's running mate in the 2000 American presidential campaign:

> I think I now have a new benchmark for 'mixed feelings.'
>
> Let's see: Orthodox Jew running for V.P. On the one hand, if this happens, Al Gore has just lost the election. I simply don't believe the country is really going to put a Jew in the White House. (I can't decide whether the next sentence should be "Especially a religious one" or "Even a religious one." Each applies, albeit to a different segment of the population.) . . .
>
> Am I cynical? A few millennia of systematic oppression can do that to a people. In a way, I'm even more scared they'll win than anything else. Just what we need to convince people that we really do run the world. As if the film industry weren't enough.[4]

Next to this entry, the epigraph is located on the left-hand margin, in a much smaller font and in verse form, and reads: "Before this night is done / Their plan will be unfurled / By the dawning of the sun / They'll take over the world ! (*Pinky and the Brain*)".

---

[3]   *Footnotes*, http://www.secraterri.com/bio.html
[4]   Shmuel's   Soapbox,   http://www.babeltower.org/soapbox/0800/080700.html   .
August 7, 2000. Accessed January 2003.

In this case, both space and contents are used in complex interaction. The marginal text is set apart from the central one by the lay-out and the use of different-sized fonts, resulting in an a-symmetrical use of space. The epigraph's contents, on the other hand, provide an apparently straightforward and therefore symmetrical comment on a tongue-in-cheek entry. Yet connoisseurs of American popular culture will have identified the source of the quotation: it is a song in a cartoon where the two characters, a cat and a mouse, make up elaborate plots to dominate the world in each episode. The contextual background therefore reinforces the rhetorical device of creating a distance between what is said and what is meant, even as it strengthens the real, implicit meaning. Here the Jewish diary-writer seemingly appropriates a common piece of anti-Semitic slander – the better to send it up, thus encouraging readers to decipher the serious undertone embedded in the lightness of his words.

Other diarists relying primarily on text create a recognizable form studded with repetitive formulae eliciting amused recognition from the readers. Terri thus writes an entry about how she watched a videotape of her children dating back to the early nineties and sent to her by her ex-husband, along with some homemade beef jerky:

> Well... it was a lot tougher than I thought it was going to be. [The Christmas video, I mean, not the beef jerky]... On the other hand, it was a lot sweeter than I expected it to be [The Christmas video, I mean, not the beef jerky]... It was definitely a lot smokier than I remembered it to be [The Christmas video, I mean, not the beef jerky]... And it was a lot more interesting, from a purely historical standpoint, than I thought it would be [The Christmas video, I mean, not the beef jerky]... On the down side, it wasn't as filling as I'd hoped it would be... But at least it wasn't as painful as I thought it would be. Usually I indulge in this sort of thing even though I know it's probably going to be hard and it's probably going to hurt and I'm probably going to be spitting blood and picking gunk out of these iffy molars of mine for the next two or three days.
> The beef jerky, I mean, not the Christmas video.[5]

The string of double-entendre ('tough, sweet, smoky, hard, hurt') builds up tension with a long list of ambiguities and misleading allusions until the punch line finally touches off in a kind of climactic resolution of tension. In the process, however, the suffering caused by

---

[5]   *Footnotes*, February 24, 2003. Accessed February 2003.

separation and loss has been hinted at, albeit in terms which could be taken at face value as well as metaphorically.

All three examples evidence that the production of humour in online diaries relies on the device of juxtaposition. When text and pictures are put side-by-side, the humorous effect may derive either from illustration, with thematically linked elements, or counterpoint, with deliberately clashing features. When images are not used, the layout of the text may function as a visual prop interacting with the meaning of the entry. In addition, the language used introduces a cognitive dissonance between signifier and signified, thus leading to laughter and at the same time indicating that the intention of the writers may be at variance with their apparent meaning. However, reducing humor to its meaning destroys laughter, as can be seen whenever anyone tries to paraphrase a joke (Szafran, Nysenholc 1994: 11-28). Formal devices are therefore essential both to producing laughter and to pointing out that there may be more to it than meets the eye. Such humor-creating devices are so prevalent in online diaries that they seem to be the indicator of an all-important, probably self-conscious function for humor in self-representational writing.

2. Functions of humor

Ever since Freud's study of jokes, (Freud 1905), followed by his article on humor (Freud 1928), the functions of humor have been understood to be those of the release of aggressive and sexual drives providing a means of saying precisely what cannot be voiced because of social or personal inhibitions. Humor thus mimes dangerous drives both as a defence against them and to better master them (Rosé 1989: 22). Thanks to language, the danger of these drives is both represented and contained. Humor, however, is far more than a mere defense: the laughter it generates shows that something which should never have been said, has nevertheless been conveyed and is right on target (Assoun 1994: 53). Humor therefore functions as a device enabling sociability, even as it gives expression to drives society would rather keep hidden. This is why humor requires the presence of a third party, even if it is only an implied ideal reader or listener, to take part in the fun (Guillaumin 1973: 637).

Because this analysis of humor acknowledges the need for an audience, it foregrounds the fact that humor has social functions, having to do with sustaining relationships: firstly, when eliciting laughter, it pinpoints the existence of a kind of common ground or interest, giving access to the innermost reaches of the Other (Assoun 1994: 54) and establishing a community (Serfaty 2002a: 82). Secondly, the shared smile or laughter is a way for humorists to get in touch with themselves or more accurately with that part of themselves that seeks to emerge to consciousness (Assoun 1994: 41). In that case, humor tends towards self-revelation and therefore also possesses clearly individual-oriented functions.

This analytical framework, when applied to online diaries, sheds light on the reasons why the self-deprecatory variety of humor is so prevalent in that particular medium. The first one is to deflect criticism: while diary writing used to be a widespread practice for religious or social purposes (Lejeune 1993), it has now become a highly individualized undertaking and contemporary diarists cannot rely on any social support for it. This is why all of them without exception feel the need to stave off criticism of their diary writing with a self-deprecatory strain of humor, which acts as a cover-up for the embarrassment of self-description and its attendant hint of ego-worship. One of the objectives of self-deprecatory humor thus is to short-circuit the criticism of others through pre-emptive striking, as can be seen from the examples quoted above. Tomato Nation and Terri make fun of themselves while Shmuel makes fun of himself, of the entire Jewish people and of the hatred some harbor against it; for all three diarists, however, the point is to take the initiative and in so doing, take away from potential attackers any enjoyment they might have derived from uttering a similar kind of witticism. Self-deprecatory humor is a way of appropriating the enjoyment of the Other and of making it one's own (Sibony 1994: 75). An additional purpose of self-deprecatory humor is to highlight that the diarist is a clear-sighted, self-aware observer of his own life, again defusing potential charges of being self-deluded. Such humor denies the existence of an originary lack within the subject and substitutes to it a somewhat contrived appearance of plenitude.

The second function of humor consists in enabling diarists to admit to painful affects. In Tomato Nation's case, the hyperbolical self-disparagement helps the writer to confront fears of rejection at birth through the disappointment she might have caused. Moreover, by assigning inhuman characteristics to her baby self, by turning her baby pictures into the very expression of otherness, she is able to sever herself from her own childhood and from her parents' desires for her and/or disappointment in her.

Similarly, Terri, in one single sentence, crams together all the sore points in her life ('non-custodial mom, recovered alcoholic'). Self-deprecatory humor enables writers to convey the hardships they are going through, even as they make light of them. Humor thus makes it possible to avoid the cloying sentimentality all too often permeating self-representational writing, a sentimentality which plunges the writers into depths of despair, without providing them with a way out. Thanks to humor, what could have been a tear-jerker is turned into a purposeful narrative of self-construction through self-revelation. Terri's diary provides just such a narration, in which humor functions first as a defence then as a device for recovery and finally as a means of intergenerational transmission, all three functions contributing to the diarist's identity construction.

3. Humor and transmission

Terri's diary *Footnotes* is self-described as "an ongoing tale of romance, recovery and uncomfortable shoes", the zeugma immediately setting a humorous tone which will be sustained throughout her autobiographical background sketch, as we saw above, and all her entries. Terri does not attempt to reach exhaustiveness in her diary; she does not stray from the subjects she has set forth to write about: she clearly has a story line and sticks to it, even while making fun of her own mannerisms, as in the entry entitled "How to write your own 'Footnotes' entry in one easy lesson", where she accurately deconstructs her own style.[6]

The carefully structured story that unfolds is that of a little girl whose mother left home to live her life and who was raised by kind maternal grandparents. Terri narrates her quiet childhood, her more turbulent adolescence and early marriage, her life as a stay-at-home mother for three children and her addiction to alcohol. She describes her discovery of Internet chat-rooms, and her love affair with a man she met online. She then details her divorce, her recovery from alcoholism and her second marriage, which led her to leave her children in her husband's custody. Her second marriage is portrayed as a blissful experience, yet it is always presented in the light, humorous tone characteristic of her entire journal.

Thanks to humor, Terri is able to let her guilt surface – her guilt over drinking or over leaving her children behind in order to live with

---

[6]   *Footnotes*, February 13, 2001. Accessed November 2002.

her second husband. But no sooner has this guilt been stated than humor appears to raise its defences; Terri never admits that the traumas of her life or of reality might have dented her conception of herself (Bergeret 1973: 557). In fact, humor helps her achieve the exact reverse: it highlights the recovery and triumph of the self, and as such it has a strong narcissistic component (Bergeret 1973: 560). Her humor achieves a compromise between the pleasure principle and the reality principle by exhibiting a degree of trust in the power of the self to be re-born (Cosnier 1973: 579).

Being online, Terri's diary has a devoted audience which responds warmly and frequently to her posts. This audience functions in complex ways, as I pointed out earlier, but I will merely argue at this point that one of its roles is to take away the guilt associated with the unorthodox life choices of the diarist, by sharing laughter directed at others, be they her former husband or her former self. Terri can thus construe her tale as one of liberation from her former marriage as well as from alcohol, and put herself in the heroic position of the woman who reinvented herself in midlife. This is evidenced by her response to a memorable email, letting her know that her journal is required reading for a college class. She comments thus:

> I've gotta [sic] admit that the idea of this website being "required reading" for a group of women in transition is a little ... unnerving. Me – the poster child for feminine dysfunction – serving as a role model? But then again, maybe I'm not a role model so much as a warning label. ("Here's what NOT to do with your life, ladies.") Either way – it's an interesting feeling. (February 24, 1999)

This passage shows the back-and-forth movement between narcissistic enjoyment of success and recognition to self-deprecatory remarks that, however, still put her in center stage, if only as a 'warning label'. The overall result is humorous enough to simultaneously constitute and conceal a strong assertion of self-worth, thus showing even more clearly the defensive role of humor and the part it can play in developing or recovering a sense of identity.

Identity, however, is a notoriously fragile construct and Terri, along with many diarists, has to balance the twin demands of autonomy and whatever inheritance has been handed down to her by her parents when trying to work out a definition of self. An entry devoted to Terri's mother's birthday is a case in point. As the narrative wanders from childhood through adolescence to adulthood, the diarist sketches a family history demonstrating how she was socialized into alcoholism and less-than-conventional motherhood, thus outlining a model of the intergenerational transmission of behavioural patterns.

Terri begins with her earliest childhood memory of her mother, then moves on to the time when her mother walked out of her marriage and left six-year-old Terri and her younger brother in her family's care. Terri reports her rejection of her mother's behavior: "All I know is this: when I grow up and become a Mama, I am never, ever going to go away and leave my children". Then the narrative skips to age thirteen, when Terri discovers her mother's diary and reads it through. Her comment: "My mom is the world's coolest mom ... I swear to god [sic]", is immediately followed by "My mom is the world's most annoying mother ... I swear to god [sic]", as she recounts her mother's break with alcoholism while Terri herself, now a mother of three, is still in the grips of the same addiction. Then the entry moves on to Terri's own break with her sixteen-year husband and her leaving behind her own three children. Finally, the narrative winds up full circle and reaches the present time, with these concluding words: "basically she [Terri's mother] is exactly what I want to be when I grow up".[7]

Both women left their families behind, both were 'non-custodial moms', both were alcoholics, both have had a diary for years: the similarities are quite striking and seem at first to be leading to mere duplication of the past. Yet nowhere do we get the impression that Terri's life is a carbon copy of her mother's. By interweaving her mother's story with her own, she indeed highlights the obvious network of correspondences between them. However, by insisting on the process of early rejection and subsequent acceptance she went through, Terri appropriates her mother's story and turns it into a force for change, rather than a drive towards repetition. What might have been a destructive pattern of iteration is made to turn into a healing, life-giving process by virtue of the light-footed humor with which the diarist glosses over the pain such a life history must have caused. In fact, Terri's telling of her mother's story within her own story amounts to a positive assertion of her place within a lineage – a matrilineal chain of transmission: after her initial rejection, she accepts her mother's inheritance and embraces their resemblances. Here, humor functions as a defence against the fear of merely

---

[7] *Footnotes,* February 25, 2001, re-entered March 27, 2002. Accessed November 2002.

repeating one's mother's life instead of being an autonomous individual.

Terri's acceptance of her mother as a model is all the more intense as the model is unconventional. She has to vindicate in her own eyes, but also in the eyes of others, the fact that she has left her children in her former husband's care, i.e., that she has deliberately flouted the motherly stereotype. This she does in a variety of ways: she mentions her guilt (March 21, 2002), her love for her drug-using daughter who is about to stand trial (March 7, 2002), thus establishing that her maternal feelings are not at fault; but she also mentions that her husband is much better than she is at taking care of the children, that he is the one who attends the hearing at the courtroom (March 9, 2002). But none of this is enough to ward off the threat of isolation or ostracism which are the usual punishments meted out to individuals who stray from conventionally acceptable behavior – here, traditional motherhood. More is needed, and this is where diary-writing comes into play: "mechanisms that allow individuals, by describing or redefining their experiences, to reconcile their own perceptions of the world with the expectations of their social groupings may have considerable value, not only to avoid such penalties, but also to handle their own inner fears. A diary can be one of these mechanisms" (Kagle, Gramegna 1996: 42). The "gentle manipulation" of reality which Terri says she engages in helps her to somewhat control if not her life itself, at least the interpretation others can have of it. Here again, the defensive role of humor is apparent, as it contributes to converting a potentially destructive deviation from social stereotypes into a success story and a validation of her choices. Humor in her diaristic narrative makes it possible for Terri both to handle her own fears of being out of line with the expectations of her social group and to rally a few others to her cause.

Interestingly, Terri grapples with the tug of war between repetition and change with her own elder daughter. Recounting in a recent entry a minor accident that happened to her daughter, she draws a parallel with an accident of her own in which a six-pack of beer landed on her toes, and writes:

> But I couldn't help it. It was the sheer poetic ludicrousness of the incident that did it. *Sticking your hand in a chicken pot pie??* That sounds like something *I* would have done at her age. [Hell. It sounds like something I would do at *MY* age.] I had to struggle for a long, painful moment to get my emotions under control before I could speak again. "Congratulations," I told her finally ... my sides aching from all that unspent mirth.

> "Your chicken pot pie beats my six-pack of root beer. No contest."
> And then we both burst into giggles.
> Daughter #1 may not have inherited my blue eyes or my bad teeth or my little round chin. She may have completely bypassed my crappy money management skills and my fondness for pseudo-reality TV shows. But there's no doubt about it: she's definitely inherited my *Stoopid Accident* gene.
> *And* my sense of humor. (Feb. 11, 2003- emphasis in the text)

Incongruity appears in the use of language: 'poetic ludicrousness' appears instead of the expected 'poetic justice', 'struggle, pain, aching' are conjoined with 'mirth'. In addition, this entry ostensibly makes fun of the notion of transmission or inheritance: it uses the rhetorical device of comic denial ("she may not have inherited…") and a reversal of meaning which turns physical flaws or imaginary ones into qualities ("my bad teeth, my fondness for reality TV, my *stoopid accident* gene"). The difference between mother and daughter is also clearly asserted ("she may have completely bypassed…") and the traits described as flaws are interspersed with compliments to the diarist ("my blue eyes, my little round chin, my sense of humor"). The narrative structure is that of the joke, with its building up of tension and its resolution in a brief punchline.

These rhetorical means show that the ostensible denunciation of her flaws amounts in fact to a celebration of herself and her elder daughter. The punch line indicates that what is really at stake is a transmission of family values through humor, the latter being of course one of these values. Therefore, in this passage as well as in the diary as a whole, self-deprecatory humor functions as a means of asserting the inter-generational link binding three generations of women through the celebration of a number of common traits, while allowing each generation its own individuality. No less importantly, the humorous mode of diary-writing also provides a socially acceptable way of publicly acknowledging one's heavy burden of guilt and ambivalence, and actualising one's potential for dynamic transmission rather than repetition.

Self-deprecatory humor in online diaries can therefore be said to possess complex functions, closely interwoven with the self-construction process diarists have long been engaging in. The protection it affords diarists enables them to bring to light habitually silent and potentially dangerous affects and drives without endangering their sense of identity. Humor makes self-revelation possible yet at the same time it offers a shelter from the doubt and division that we all labor under and which, should they come to light, might endanger our narcissistic feeling of wholeness. Self-deprecatory humor therefore does not tend towards subversion or transgression but allows the self to sustain the buffeting of life and to emerge unscathed. As such, it is particularly adapted to the hybrid of private and public selves emerging in online diaries.

Chapter Four

The Private – Public Divide

The contemporary appetite for intimate disclosure is hardly a recent phenomenon. It can be said to date back at least as far as the pre-Romantic era and Jean-Jacques Rousseau's *Confessions* (1788). By projecting intimate events onto the public sphere, Rousseau testified to a need to unveil the intimate truths of the self through writing – a need that has endured up to the present time. Evolution does occur, however, in that the dividing line between public and private selves is negotiated differently in different societies at different historical periods (Petitat 2001), making it necessary to re-think the location of this divide.

In contemporary industrialized societies, the desire for transparency permeates political and social discourse as part of a vast ideological formation, so that the public and the private sphere seem to meld and merge, much to the dismay of many. But the contemporary permeability of the public and the private is not necessarily catastrophic. As will become clear in this chapter, the ceaseless back and forth movement between the two realms transforms the drive towards huddling over one's secrets and hoarding them into a circulation between the individual and the collective. The Internet opens up the closed space of interiority onto a space that is far larger than itself, without being totally public, however.

1. Publicizing the intimate

As regards the private or public nature of diaries, attitudes have widely varied over time. While Samuel Pepys wrote coded entries mixing several languages in order to conceal his sex life, and Boswell's Journal was so well hidden that it was not found until two centuries later, the situation seems to have changed in the nineteenth century. Oscar Wilde for instance, in *The Importance of Being Earnest*, derides the way in which young society ladies envision their diaries:

> Algernon: Do you really keep a diary ? I'd give anything to look at it. May I ?
>
> Cecily: Oh no. You see, it is simply a very young girl's record of her own thoughts and impressions, and consequently meant for publication. When it appears in volume form I hope you will order a copy. (Wilde 1930: 377; quoted by Rosenwald 1988: 8).

Similarly, Rosenwald describes the social use of the diary in nineteenth-century Concord: journals were presented to mere acquaintances, who then offered theirs for reading in return, prompting a comparison between reading other people's diaries and "paying a social call" (Rosenwald 1988: 77). The spiritual journals kept by young girls in the nineteenth century had to be shown to their parents or religious mentors. Diaries have also been put to pedagogical, and hence quite public uses in nineteenth century feminine education (Lejeune 1993; Simonet-Tenant 2001: 54). This still goes on nowadays, as evidenced by the testimony of one diarist: "When I was a freshman in college, I had to write in my journal every day for English class, and I still have that journal. I tried to pick writing topics instead of writing mundane details of my daily life, so that makes it even more interesting".[1] Both nineteenth-century and contemporary examples therefore show that the private nature of diaries can by no means be taken for granted, especially considering the fact that many were routinely published.

1.1. Writing for an implicit audience

In an even more fundamental way, diaries may be said to contain an implicit reader within their very writing process. As already emphasized in an earlier chapter, revisions and explanatory notes contextualizing the people interacting with the diarist point to the presence of an, at the very least implied, reader or fictional addressee (Iser 1976). In Lynn Bloom's words, truly private diaries "are so terse

---

[1] *Lisa's Journey*, March 7, 2002.
http://web.archive.org/web/20010810174127/http://www.section12.com/users/lisa_p/.
Accessed March 2002.

they seem coded. No reader outside the author's immediate society or household could understand them without extra-textual information; [...] observations are elliptical, places and people are not identified, events are not interpreted; it is an *aide-mémoire* [...] using a page-a-day pre-printed memorandum book" (Bloom 1996: 25-26). In addition, diarists themselves write with later reading in mind. Gusdorf states that although diaries may be meant to be read by a variety of people, the very first addressees are the diarists themselves (Gusdorf 1991a: 391). Lejeune concurs with this view and says: "from the outset, a diary is planned for re-reading. [...] It is not envisioned as a *finished* object, but as a text that will eventually be *re-read* either by oneself or by some other reader" (Lejeune 2000a: 213).[2] Contemporary media and the Internet may therefore be said not only to prolong an age-old trend, but also to conform to the underlying, inner structure of diaries.

Still, the power of the myth endures. Pierre Pachet for instance begins his study of diaristic writing by asserting that it is "by definition meant to be hidden" (Pachet 2001: 7).[3] The prevalence of this view is such that publicizing the intimate seems to arouse questioning both among people who publish their diary online, and among readers of online diaries. Diarists go ahead and write anyway, but try to explain and vindicate their reasons for doing so publicly. Moreover, they attempt to maintain a modicum of privacy by setting up limits to their revelations and by placing cautionary warnings in the incipit to ward off the intrusion of unwanted readers.

1.2. Diarists and family members

Many writers thus include in the preamble to the entries proper their misgivings about the journal being read by family members or acquaintances, because they might, in Shmuel's words, "learn more than [they] would want to know"[4]. Another diarist, Bitter Hag, writes:

> If you know me in real life, then chances are you've stumbled
> on this site by accident. There's a reason I didn't give you this
> URL. I say this because this is where I do a lot of my venting
> about things I see and people I encounter in everyday life. If

---

[2]   "Dès le départ, il est programmation de sa relecture. [...] On ne l'imagine pas *fini*, on le voit plutôt *relu* (par soi) ou lu (par autrui) ".

[3]   "Les écrits dont nous parlons, par définition, sont écrits pour ne pas se manifester, pour être cachés".

[4]   *Shmuel's Soapbox*, "Index", http://www.babeltower.org/soapbox/ . Accessed September 2001 and *seq.*.

> you are one of those people, you are likely to get your feelings
> hurt. It would be best for all concerned if you'd just turn
> around and leave now.[5]

Shmuel issues dire warnings to members of his family or to
acquaintances who might stumble upon his diary, writing:

> (In the unlikely event that anybody in my family has stumbled
> across this journal, and somehow missed the prominent *"Go
> Away"* message on the front page, let me reiterate: the stuff
> here doesn't concern you, and if you read on anyway, and I
> find out, I *will* make your life a living hell. And that goes for
> any entry, not just this one. Scram. Thank you.)[6]

These two examples show that what some diarists fear to reveal is
neither a dark sexual secret nor drug abuse, say, but their own hostility
to their relatives or acquaintances: this is their most burdensome
secret, this is what they are unable to openly take responsibility for,
because such hostility towards family invokes fear and denial in the
subject. They ask family members who might chance upon their
journals to leave, because this is the best way for them to preserve
peace or the status quo and thus to avoid a conflict they are as yet
unable to handle.

Here as elsewhere, however, ambivalence is the rule. Shmuel, for
instance, who asserts he wants his family not to read his weblog, still
provides his own name and the address of his 'official' web page,
albeit hidden deep in the recesses of his diary.[7] Moreover, an incident
described in full in his diary illustrates his complex attitude regarding
the public-private divide: shortly after beginning his online diary, his
grandmother's death led him to compose an entry in her memory.
What followed is both comical and characteristic of the ambivalence
regarding the publicizing of private writings:

> I then, for whatever reason – I've given up trying to
> understand the way my mind works sometimes – printed out a
> copy of the January 24th entry for myself, nicely reformatted
> to fit on a page in three columns, with no direct evidence that
> this was anything but a page from my personal, private diary.
> And, yes, I suppose I knew that I was going to show it to
> somebody else, and that it would be utterly stupid to do so.

---

5   Bitter Hag, http://www.bitterhag.com/index.asp . Accessed January 2003.
6   *Shmuel's Soapbox*, June 2, 2002 entry.
http://www.babeltower.org/soapbox/blog/2002_06_02_old.html. Emphasis in the text.
7   http://www.babeltower.org/soapbox/surveys.html, *op. cit.*

> [...] I did, of course. My aunt. Who proceeded to show it to
> my grandfather and my uncle, and, well, I think the entire
> family tree is going to get their hands on the thing before long.
> [...] *I'd thought the danger was outside discovery. Ha. We
> have met the enemy, and he is us.* [...] Thankfully, nobody
> asked why – if I was writing this as an entry in my personal
> journal – it was clearly written for an audience that didn't
> know any of the participants. I didn't name anybody, I
> explained a relationship or two along the way... it was pretty
> clearly not a normal diary entry.[8]

Keenly aware of all the issues of contextualization and publicity
surrounding diaristic practises, Shmuel still gives in to the writerly
impulse of communicating his work to others, even to family
members who may (and do) object to it, thus illustrating the kinship
between fear of disclosure and desire for it. Such misadventures may
also indicate the social limits to openness in a given social group –
limits which diarists trespass at their own risk. In other words,
revealing the intimate never goes without saying, nor can one reveal
the same thing to everyone.

1.3. Ordinariness

Another frequent issue when publicizing one's journal is that of the
intrinsic interest of one's life for prospective readers, as appears from
the following example:

> I started to write an entry all about my Thanksgiving non-
> adventures, but that fell into the dual categories of "Boring as
> hell" and "No one gives a flying fuck". So instead, I decided to
> chronicle a couple of recent developments - three that had me
> all a-twitter, and one that pissed me off royally. I suspect they
> still fall under "Boring as hell" and "No one gives a flying
> fuck", but if you really get down to it, this whole journal falls
> smack dab right into the middle of those, so I just quit
> worrying about it and wrote this anyway.[9]

In this case, the diarist is grappling with her own sense of
worthlessness, far more than with any neutral evaluation of her own
life. It is interesting to note that, when saying that her life is boring,
this writer includes in her reasoning the reader and hence the public
nature of her writing. By dismissing the entire issue of "boring vs.
interesting" entries and unreservedly accepting the ordinariness of her

---

[8]   *Shmuel's Soapbox, op. cit.,* January 26, 1999. Emphasis added.
[9]   Bitter Hag, December 9, 2003, http://www.bitterhag.com/current.asp.

experience, this diarist is affirming her determination to ground value in herself rather than in others. She also purely and simply chooses to disregard the effects that the public character of her writing may have on the audience. Other diarists, however, have moved far beyond this position and address the question of the public-private divide with an altogether different attitude.

2. Repercussions of self-revelation

2.1. Effects on the individual in society

Analyzing his own production process, Miles Hochstein thus writes in *Documented Life:* "I admit that I have sought to avoid overtly embarrassing myself, or others. I have wrestled with the right balance between exposure and privacy. In my life there are at least a few things better left unsaid, and certainly a number of moments better forgotten. (You too? Yeah, I hear you. Join the club.) I try to be nice to people here. I'm not into settling accounts."

'Niceness' immediately evokes behavior codes, social etiquette and self-censorship. Because his diary is public, Miles seems to recoil from any infringement on established social codes. Indeed, making one's diary public from the outset might condemn the writer to rigid adherence to social codes. Being completely transparent to others, being subjected to maximum visibility can lead to so strong an internalization of social conventions that writers can textualize nothing but the most conventional feelings, actions or thoughts (Foucault 1975: 236).

This indeed happens in those diaries expressly written to provide onlookers with a record of daily activities. Each entry displays nothing but a socially acceptable version of the self, devoid of any controversial or negative aspect. In acting thus, diarists attempt to repress and suppress whatever is unsayable, unnameable. Diaristic writing then turns into another cover-up, both protecting inner life and carefully hiding it from view. There may sometimes be a very thin line between such protection and less than full truthfulness. The prevailing blandness of such diaries points to the harshness of the normative social gaze, as well as to the fact that a diary by no means necessarily entails self-disclosure or a re-negotiation of privacy. Such texts merely secularize the religious diary young girls had to keep in the nineteenth century and show to their parents on a daily basis as evidence of their religious purity. They act as metonymies for the self in society and hence do not attempt anything but a record of the trivia daily life is made of.

At first sight, this seems to be the case in *Documented Life*. The blend of text and pictures looks remarkably like a family album, uncontroversial and reassuring – until we come to the second part of the preamble, where Miles thinks through the concept of living a "documented life":

> Why do we instinctively know that we must hide ourselves and our lives if we are to survive? Is this knowledge of the supposed 'need' to hide really knowledge, or is it an illusion? Who benefits if we are afraid of revealing our own stories? Who benefits from our fears? Should we allow the fears we have about being known, seen, watched, or observed to control our lives, or might there be value in freeing ourselves from our fears of being seen?
>
> In the 21st century we are witness to "cam-girls" (and cam-guys? and autodocumenters?) who live their lives online, and to bloggers who report their daily activities and musings. The idea of not being hidden, or of breaking down the normal barriers to privacy, is in play. What they may share with this web site is an interest in being rebelliously indifferent to observation. We are all engaged in resisting the idea that we are disempowered by being seen, or that we can only find empowerment by being private. Some of us even suspect that the need for privacy plays right into the dominance structures that are predicated upon one way observation. We are perhaps fighting the use of observation as a technique of power, by claiming the status of "being observed" as a way of empowering ourselves, and thus of dismantling the use of one way observation to dominate and shame and control.

This highly perceptive text displays a keen awareness of the issues at stake: the socially constructed distrust of narrative self-exposure is identified and clearly linked to the matter of control; the contemporary phenomenon of people choosing to film their lives and publicize it on the Internet is interpreted as a rebellion against social control and as a way of regaining power over their own lives. Publicly exposing one's privacy turns into a radical criticism of society. Paradoxically, however, even though for the diarist under consideration the transgression of secrecy may be fraught with socially altering and ultimately empowering implications, his own diary remains well within the social strictures on self-disclosure.

How can this vindication of self-revelation be reconciled with the limits to openness set in the earlier part of the preamble ? Of course it cannot be. But precisely because these opposing views cannot be reconciled, they point to the split between opposite drives within the self. Fear of transparency does battle with the desire for total self-disclosure, and diaristic writing is a means of resolution of this conflict. By taking up the simultaneous position of observer and observed, "what the diary material forces is a recognition of a gap – a space within which, in the process of both embodying and representing self, an irony, a distance […] can happen (Pini 2000)". Therefore the long-range goal – creating social change through self-disclosure – serves as self-justification to the potentially unsettling self-scrutiny that a diary inevitably involves as it directs the subject towards that part of himself that he represses and wants nothing to do with, but that keeps trying to gain admittance to his consciousness.

The tug-of-war between opposing drives is not necessarily found in all diaries. Some, like Carolyn Burke, hold firm beliefs in the value of total honesty. In a diary attempting a representation of the inner processes of the self, she simultaneously posits and violates the existence of a private domain, as she thrusts further back the boundaries of what can be revealed. In the preamble to her journal, reproduced on the Online Diary History site, she thus writes:

> I believed strongly in the power of good that results from free expression, free information exchange, and open and honest communication between people. I'd been studying Popper and Feyerabend in university, about creating an open society as one aspect in the pursuit of better quality knowledge.
>
> An online diary, a place that exposed private mental spaces to everyone's scrutiny seemed like a social obligation to me. I felt at the time that I could give back to society something important: a snapshot of what a person is like on the inside. This is something that we don't get access to in face to face, social society. Out intimacies are hidden, and speaking of them in public is taboo.
>
> I questioned the privacy taboo. I disagreed with it. I exposed my private and intimate world to public awareness. *"How dare you display your private diary to the world on purpose".* [10]

Like Miles Hochstein, Carolyn Burke very clearly attributes social functions to the invasion of her own privacy she engages in, as well as

---

[10]   http://www.diaryhistoryproject.com/recollections/1995_01_03.htm. Italics in the text.

being aware of the fact that she is breaking a taboo. Trying to uncover the truth about oneself pre-supposes a general logic whereby appearances rule. Therefore the private quest for truth inevitably collides with social rules. This is why diarists think their utter honesty might have revolutionary repercussions. They are aware, however dimly, of the socially transgressive nature of their candor.

2.2. Effects on the individual and language

There is, however, more to this. The drive to expose one's physical or psychological privacy meets other, not necessarily social needs. For one thing, the desire for total openness, so much at variance with the construction of a fictional self one necessarily carries out when writing a diary, corresponds to a subconscious wish to return to the universe of unfettered communication and mutual comprehension supposedly marred by shame and by social conventions. The most fascinating diaries indeed move beyond the social self to give the reader/viewer a glimpse of the depths. They meet the deep-set human desire for transparency deriving from the realization that communicating the immediacy of one's own experience is impossible to achieve once childhood has been left behind (Starobinski 1971: 19). The consequence of such incommunicability is closure in the opacity of self, while the desire for unity with the Other turns into a desire for instantaneous understanding, going together with the fantasy of a Golden Age: a mythical beginning where unity ruled, where no veil whatsoever came between one and the Other.

This quest for untrammelled communication inevitably comes up against the obstacle of language, because the primary characteristic of language is the multiplicity of meaning and its echoes with the unconscious processes of the reader/viewer. Language fundamentally contains a dialectic of transparency and opacity that is the very foundation of its value. In Michel Foucault's words, "the signifier is not supposed to 'translate' without concealing and without leaving the signified with inexhaustible reserves of meaning; the signified only unveils itself in the visible world, laden with a signifier that is itself fraught with a meaning it does not control" (Foucault 1993: xii-xiii).[11] To take up again the initial metaphor this study is exploring, language in and of itself veils what it conveys with layer upon layer of meaning. Unveiling the multiple significance of language, the diarist or the

---

[11]   "Le signifiant n'est pas censé 'traduire' sans cacher, et sans laisser le signifié dans une inépuisable réserve; le signifié ne se dévoile que dans le monde visible, et lourd d'un signifiant chargé lui-même d'un sens qu'il ne maîtrise pas".

reader only finds another veil. Even supposing that full transparency and perfect understanding were ever achieved, this would result in the foundering of language, whose usefulness would come to an end. Diary writing is therefore predicated on a search for meaning and for transparency that is fully aware of its own impossibility.

Another reason why diaries keep on being published on the Internet is that, by communicating about their inner lives, diarists are not merely engaging in self-expression, but are actually trying to better appropriate some elements of their own lives by theatricalizing them through words and pictures. Although self-dramatization may sound like another impediment to total openness, it actually helps externalize inner processes and display them to others in the hope that they will respond, so that they can be internalized anew, in modified form. This externalization of one's intimate life is what Jacques Lacan, followed by many others, called 'extimacy'.[12] The drive toward self-revelation is thus one of the means through which individuals attempt to gain better access to their inner life.

3. Names and pseudonyms

Interestingly, some diarists provide their actual names, like Miriam H. Nadel or Miles Hochstein.[13] The use of one's real name possesses important connotations and constitutes another indication of the role played by self-representational writing in the assertion of a reconstructed 'I'. One's name being both a sign and a guarantee of one's identity, its appearance in the preamble or 'about' section of a diary constitutes the writer's first foray into self-construction. In addition, when writing under their real-life names, diarists attempt to alter the rules governing social communication by blurring or pushing back the boundaries of what can be disclosed, and what has to be withheld from others (Lejeune 2000b: 422). In other words, privacy is acknowledged, but only so as to be invaded and thus to evade the strict social control enjoining us to hide certain facts of our lives from certain people or from the world at large. This more particularly concerns the revelations regarding sexuality; when communication is or becomes impossible with family members and acquaintances

---

[12]   This is a word coined to translate the French coinage 'extimité'. See for instance Tisseron 2001: 52; Assoun 1995: 48; see also Simonet-Tenant 2001: 11, quoting Michel Tournier's use of the same word.
[13]   *Areas of Unrest, op. cit.*; *Documented Life, op. cit.*

regarding sexual mores or orientation, the public diary may be a passive-aggressive way of being found out by accident/on purpose.

Contrary to appearances, the use of a pseudonym does not really go against the trend toward greater self-revelation. For one thing, pseudonyms are often accompanied by pictures that add the density of corporeity to the diaristic text and potentially enable identification by family or acquaintances. Pseudonyms therefore are hardly effective in concealing the identity of the writer even while they are ostensibly being used for this purpose. In addition, pseudonyms are often chosen in order to actualise some of the psychological traits the writer cannot vent anywhere and may thus acquire considerable expressiveness. That the self-chosen names or pseudonyms may become significant metonymies of the self refers to ancient practises analysed by Horkheimer and Adorno: "the name [...] turns into an arbitrary and pliable label whose efficiency may be calculated, but precisely as a result of this, it acquires the despotic force of the archaic name" (Horkheimer, Adorno 1974: 173).[14] In other words, the pseudonym is endowed with an expressive function which links it to primeval beliefs about the metonymical link between the phonemes of the name and the bearer. Far from being a sign merely referring to a specific person without being in and of itself endowed with meaning, the pseudonym becomes a decipherable element which exposes the qualities and specificities of the fictional avatar each diarist develops thanks to self-representational writing. This happens partly because, in social representations, the Internet is strongly associated with the idea of virtual community. Using a pseudonym might therefore signal that one is now entering a distinct universe, in which different rules apply, and where one's personality may develop to the full. In other words, both the real name and the pseudonym fulfil similar functions in online diaries.

4. The case of erotic diaries

The sex blogs and erotic diaries identified by a Google search are often commercial sites posing as personal ones. This is the case whenever a password or some sort of registration is required for entry, as is the case for SuicideGirls.com, for instance, where members have to contribute a small fee and amateur nude models are paid if their

---

[14] "Le nom [...] se transforme en étiquette arbitraire et manipulable dont on peut calculer l'efficacité, mais elle acquiert de ce fait même la force despotique du nom archaïque".

pictures are selected to appear on the site.[15] There is no dearth of
personal diaries primarily devoted to sex, however, but they tend to
fall into specialized categories, such as "polyamory", referring to open
relationships[16], gay, lesbian and transgender relationships,[17] or
BDSM.[18] A very large number of sex-oriented weblogs began in the
summer of 2003, suggesting a fad spurred on by the media coverage
about weblogs, which intensified at approximately that time. Many of
these self-described erotic weblogs are little more than repetitive
descriptions or more probably, and often avowedly, fantasies of sexual
episodes. Devoid of any hint of detail about the writer, such weblogs
feature no picture gallery and provide very few specifics even in the
sex scenes, which remain largely abstract.[19] Diary writers themselves
complain about their dullness: "Not enough character. Not enough
sizzle *between* the two characters. Not enough pacing – here's what
she looks like (36-24-36), here's what he looks like (6 pack, dreamy
eyes), oh my god his cock her pussy pump pump pump. [...] Yawn".[20]
Such writings are closer to pornography than to eroticism in that they
aim at titillating the reader by the use of certain coded, supposedly
taboo words, resulting in a curiously disembodied sexuality.
Repetitive in lay-out and content, their recent *en masse* creation
probably points to a loosening of the stigma and reprobation
surrounding auto-eroticism.

Other, less monotonous diaries were started much earlier and mix
accounts of daily life with depictions of sex scenes in varying ratios.
Breakup Babe, for instance, describes the life of a thirty-something
software engineer in full detail, up to and including a comical
recapitulation of all her dates for the year 2003.[21] The sexual
revelations remain euphemistic, which reinforces their humorous tone.
But the self-disclosure fully functions as an attractor, eliciting a large
number of comments from readers. Similarly, *Meditations of a Sweet
Jezebel* contains a 'sex meter' reading: "It's been fifty-one days since

[15] http://suicidegirls.com/tour/ . Accessed December 2003.
[16] For instance, *Naked Loft Party*, http://www.nakedloftparty.blogspot.com/ or *Blog in A-flat minor*, http://www.frondle.net/blog/ . Accessed November 2003.
[17] Debra Hydes's *Pursed Lips*, http://www.pursedlips.com, Accessed January 2003.
[18] Bondage, domination, sadism and masochism, http://www.section12.com.
[19] See for instance DeeGee Girl Diary, http://deegeegirl.blogspot.com/ , or the portal to sex blogs and sex news maintained by Daze Reader, http://www.dazereader.com/weblog.htm . Accessed December 2003.
[20] *Her Desires*, November 26, 2003, http://www.herdesires.net/archives/diary/20031126_on_erotica.html.
[21] *Breakup Babe*, December 24, 2003 entry, http://breakupbabe.blogspot.com/ .

Jezebel has had carnal relations".[22] The entries give ample details about the writer's relationships, yet remain within the bounds of a certain propriety; four-letter words are written with a coy asterisk replacing one of the letters, euphemism veils many of the incidents, recalling the writing style of the feminine print press.

Nevertheless, the weblogs providing room for the depiction of sexual experiences may be said to be erotic not so much because they strive for artistic effect, but because they attempt to mesh the intimate and the social parts of their lives, so as to give a more palpable, embodied quality to their private lives. Eroticism indeed derives part of its disturbing or alluring power because it openly displays what is supposed to remain hidden. Eroticism publicizes the private and the intimate, challenging in the process a number of social and sexual norms. This is probably the reason why diaristic narratives possess more than an anecdotal link with erotic texts, since writing openly about sex may be designated as a specific example of the exposure self-representational writing tends to. Unsurprisingly, therefore, erotic diaries abound on the Internet, running the gamut of all sexual orientations, as becomes apparent from even a casual search.

Given this definition of eroticism, how can it be distinguished from pornography, which also disturbs and entices through disclosure? One possible answer, evidenced by the sex blogs themselves when they establish a clear distinction between personal and pornographic blogs,[23] is that pornography emanates from an industry, and hence is defined by the rules of any profit-making organization. Another possibility is that such diaries differ from pornography in that they do not produce "an abstraction of human intercourse in which the self is reduced to its formal elements [...] [and] people to mammals" (Carter 1978: 4). Unlike pornography which usually unfolds in abstract places – unnamed cities or generic countryside – erotic diarists ground their writing in well-defined environments and provide context about the writer and whoever interacts with him or her. Full particulars are given for each diarist, and photo galleries are just as well-stocked as in more traditional diaries. In weblogs, writing about sexuality is an essential part of the self-construction entailed by diaristic practices.

Erotic diaries push to its limit the principle that self-revelation is inherently a conscious or unconscious seduction technique. The openly stated purpose is to attract readers, sometimes in a competition

---

[22] *Meditations of a Sweet Jezebel*, December 22, 2003 entry, http://wickedjezebel.blogspot.com.
[23] See for instance the classification of links on Daze Reader's site, *op. cit.*

to obtain a higher rank in the popularity ratings regularly published by site managers. The implicit purposes of erotic self-representational writing reach, however, far deeper than this.

First, as we shall see in more detail in one of the following chapters, the technological apparatus of the computer seems to euphemize the materiality of the body; hidden by the screen and the keyboard, represented only by text or digital portraits, the body becomes the representation of a representation, in other words, an abstraction at the *nth* power. Being seemingly denied, corporeity therefore reasserts itself through the foregrounding of the body in erotic scenes, on the one hand, and through the eroticization of writing on the other hand. Writing extends and prolongs sexual episodes, which are then enjoyed twice, once in the doing, and once in the telling. Erotic diary writing can thus become a substitute for absent sex and an erotic activity of its own.

Secondly, straightforward depictions of standard sexual practices appear to be far less common than representations of marginalized sexual tastes and orientations, the most common kink being domination and submission. When such diarists try to spell out their reasons for writing, what often emerges is an attempt at vindicating their perceived marginality. Therefore these weblogs may be said to function as tools to negotiate and construct the contours of selves that have chosen to be outside the boundaries of social acceptability and are therefore often regarded as phenomena rather than people. The public discourse about the personal experience of marginal sexuality helps to break down social stereotypes on the one hand, and on the other hand to promote a degree of self-acceptance. This paradoxically works through the assumption of social stereotypes, rather than their rejection. The names of the weblogs very often bespeak the tendency to identify with negative representations about oneself: "bj's [sic] gay porno-crazed ramblings", for instance, or "Salacity and Scurrility" are among the tamer, albeit illustrative examples.[24]

Erotic diaries therefore can hardly make a claim for social subversion, because they thrive on the existence of taboos and on their continued power over the psyche of a large number of people. Nudity, whether of the body or of the writing, starts by assaulting the reader's internalised sense of propriety or, in psycho-analytical terms, the Super-ego, and proceeds to batter the defences erected around privacy, apparently triumphing over them. Yet it quickly hits the limits any

---

[24]   Links provided by Daze Reader, *op. cit.*

human activity has to contend with, the limits of representation and the limits of language. The close-up shots of sexual organs pornographic pictures favor, ultimately preserve the silence and muteness of the flesh, while the most prolix depictions of sensual desire and fulfilment still and inevitably maintain the veil of language over the perceived experience. Erotic diaries and weblogs strive towards total representation, but their attempts, fortunately, always leave something to be desired.

Chapter Five

Male and Female Cyberbodies

Online diaries perpetuate a long tradition of self-representational writing even as they modify it structurally. The structural changes driven by technology indeed create a new set of expectations and of writing practises, yet they do not alter one of the major foci of diary writing, i.e., the process of identity construction which numerous critics, starting with Gusdorf in 1956 and up to the present day, have found to be at the core of self-representational writings (Gusdorf 1956: 106-123). Taking this finding as its departure point, the present chapter will attempt to analyze the ways in which corporeity is involved in identity formation in online journals. Working against the assumption that the body and more broadly speaking corporeity play no part in the development of online identities, this chapter proposes to look into the intersection of the body, gender and cyberspace in a number of Internet diaries.

1. Disembodied in cyberspace

Science-fiction author William Gibson coined the word 'cyberspace' to refer to a two-tiered set-up including on the one hand, a system connecting men and computers and projecting a "disembodied consciousness into the consensual hallucination that [is] the matrix" (Gibson 1984: 11), and on the other hand the matrix itself, which is a set of interlinked databases scattered all over the world and containing "bright lattices of logic unfolding across the colourless void" (Gibson 1984: 11). Since, in his fictional world, human consciousness can be accommodated by computers, corporeity seemingly becomes redundant. The hero of *Neuromancer*, Case, keeps referring to his body as "meat", thus underscoring the contempt in which his society holds the body (Gibson 1984: 12). Other science-fiction writers depict mostly dystopian worlds shunning corporeity (Asimov 1954).

This fictional fascination with radicalizing the mind/body divide is widely echoed in social sciences. Drawing on the fantasies designed by science-fiction writers, the earliest commentators on the Internet, be they philosophers, sociologists or pro-Internet activists, view it as a technology liable to end up in separating human beings from their body – for some, a consummation devoutly to be wished; many in fact believe that the peculiar technological arrangement governing the use of the Internet can end up in the creation of "angelic bodies" (Lévy 1994), reminiscent of medieval views "of a psychosomatic individual from which the psycho part can be separated and inhabit cyberspace in its new virtual body with which it can interact with other virtual 'angelic' bodies" (Fisher 1996). For many writers, such as Internet activist John Perry Barlow, the body's loss of materiality is supposed to lead to under-emphasizing gender, class and race, thus paving the way for a utopian world of idealized interpersonal relationships, free from the taint of social or sexual discrimination (Barlow 1996).

Underneath the desire for disembodiment and the idealistic statement of purpose, there lurks the age-old disgust for and distrust of the body. The fundamental negativity of this stance derives from the very nature of the body: "being linked to flesh, matter, decay and hence to the deathbound destruction wrought by time, [...] the body [...] refers back to nothingness" (Brohm 1988: 22-23).[1] The anxiogenic body is best left behind or negated, a position sanctioned by a long philosophical tradition initiated by Plato in *Phedon* and *Phaedra*. There is a clear metaphysical hierarchy separating the soul from the body, placing one far above the other, and interpreting their conjunction in a reprehensible light.

Conversely, the mind/body dichotomy seemingly stemming from and amplified by the use of modern computer technology strikes fear in other, more technophobic commentators (Benedikt 1991; Le Breton 1999). In a lyrical expression of dismay, media theoretician Régis Debray describes the dire consequences of disembodiment: "the intellectual art of digital simulation makes nerves and muscles redundant. [...] We have no more contact with anything material. The mind has freed itself from the hand, the whole body has turned into

---

[1]   "Situé du côté de la chair, de la matière, de la déchéance, et donc du temps destructeur qui aboutit à la mort [...] le corps [...] renvoie au néant".

calculus, the earth has been left behind, ushering in mind-boggling freedom – and the toll exacted from us is loss of desire" (Debray 1992: 304-305).[2]

The phobia triggered by the computer logically extends to the Internet. In cyberspace, corporeity seemingly dissolves and boils down to a set of linguistic signs. The body's metamorphosis into text, the perceived immateriality of the flesh eventually turn it into a sheer signifier; like money in Karl Marx's famous definition, the body-as-text is a kind of 'general equivalent' with connotations of both uniformity and universality, thus causing it to lose its uniqueness as well as its value as a fixed social symbol. By stretching the money metaphor a bit further, the body-as-text, like an overabundance of paper money, arouses fears of symbolical devaluation. Inflation is indeed devastating for both currency and corporeity.

Furthermore, viewing the body as an immaterial signifier, as a set of linguistic signs, entails that it is an empty form, without any pre-set content; because of this very emptiness, it is full of all possible meanings. The self-conscious and deliberate textualisation of the body underscores its function as a representation, open to a multiplicity of interpretations, a multiplicity of meanings. The body-as-text is viewed as inherently polysemous, but this very polysemy generates deep anxiety, because it is viewed as liable to undermine the stability of the representations of the body – a situation ultimately leading to the dissolution of the body politic. Disaster in the public sphere is thus predicted as a result of expelling corporeity from the scene of representation on the Internet or through the use of computers (Serfaty 1999: 174).

2. Embodied in cyberspace

Like all new communication technologies, the Internet has given rise to both utopian and dystopian interpretations, all of which, however, observation consistently fails to vindicate (Serfaty 2000: 231-241). In fact, and contrary to what early writers either hoped for or feared, the perceived abstractness and immateriality of the Internet may even have resulted in obsessively foregrounding the body; this is

---

[2]   " La simulation numérique, cet art de tête, met les nerfs et les muscles au chômage. [...] Plus de contact avec une matière. L'esprit s'est libéré de la main, le corps entier devient calcul, on a décollé de la terre. Liberté fabuleuse, payée de la perte du désir".

perhaps one of the reasons why the Internet, like its Minitel[3] forebear, opens up unlimited vistas for pornography and its disquieting representations of corporeity.   Even without resorting to such specialized expressions of embodiment, observation indeed shows that in online diaries, the body and more generally the material world, far from being left behind, keep cropping up in diverse ways. Even when the body is apparently absent, as when the diarists mourn their loneliness or the end of their relationships, this lack is the very basis of a reflection on corporeity.

However, because corporeity is a perceptual reality but a fluid concept, a tentative definition of what is meant here by this notion is in order. Corporeity may be said to gain prominence whenever descriptions of significant events involving the body and sexuality are included, but also through the introduction of pictures of the writers, of their surroundings and of the world at large. The definition of corporeity this study rests on therefore encompasses not only the way the writers perceive their own bodies, but also the way they perceive their surroundings, as well as the palpable reality of the diary itself, its frames, its division into several screens, the division of each screen into different sections. Many diarists indeed comment on their HTML code or on the difficulties inherent in maintaining a site.[4] Introducing the perception of the material world and of the materiality of the journal is a way of going beyond the traditional mind/body divide and of placing embodied experience at the theoretical core of this analysis.

The material world is chiefly rendered through pictures meshing with the text to a variety of effects. Inserting pictures within diaries is not specific to the Internet – the medium merely enhances the whole process, providing vividness as well as the interactivity of hypertext, enabling the reader to either click the links leading to the pictures or forego them altogether. The pictures of physical locations, of various objects taken from the writer's environment, of the writers themselves or of the people closest to them all meet a similar need: because a diary is by definition stamped with discontinuity, because it is fragmented into a myriad narratives in discontinuous entries, the representations of body and of space function first as devices of

---

[3]   Minitel was a precursor of the Internet introduced solely in France in the late nineteen seventies.

[4]   See for instance *Shmuel's Soapbox, op. cit.*, January 21 & 27, 1999, or *Aiyah's Net, op. cit.*, "Site Basics", http://www.aiyah.net/backbone.htm . Accessed January 2002.

continuity, geared to enhancing narrativity, and therefore giving both diarist and reader a framework helping to order experience.

In addition, chronologically arranged pictures provide a sense of the passage of time, a time frame which also contributes to strengthening narrativity. The events of daily life are forced into a narrative mold which, when looked at in a long-term perspective, infuses the diary with either the sense of a progression or of stagnation, hence furthering the fictionalisation process at work in journals. Finally, representations of body and of space function as devices of both expansion and repetition, producing and bolstering meaning, inasmuch as diarists seek absolute transparency and hence attempt to render their personal experience from as many angles as possible. This is the reason why the self-portrait embedded in a space already devoted to self-representational writing is far from being redundant; it repeats and reinforces what the written text already delineates, thus striving towards a complete rendering of experience.

Yet even as it does so, the self-portrait merely adds another layer of visual meaning to the textualisation of self, so that transparency recedes even further away. The textual and graphic representations of the body, of the material world and more generally speaking of corporeity, although striving for transparency, in fact interplay to produce a narrative of self, a construct, rather than the hoped for, unmediated, essential truth about the diarist. This is intrinsic to self-representational writing and already perceived to be so by one of its earliest practitioners, Jean-Jacques Rousseau (Starobinski 1971: 224), but it is also due to the nature of language, which is both the locus of immediate experience and a medium. Language enables "the representation of an authentic self, while at the same time revealing that perfect truth has yet to be attained" (Starobinski 1971: 238-239). However, even if the self is only a construct of language, it is one of the necessary fictions individuals base their lives upon.

3. Corporeity, image and text

3.1. Portraits

The two diaries which will be examined in the course of this section were chosen for the widely dissimilar personalities of their authors, in an attempt at pointing up the structural similarities between their diaristic narratives. Bunt Sign[5] is a middle-aged man who works

---

[5]   http://www.buntsign.com/index.html Quotations from this diary will be identified by the letters *BS* and the entry date.

from home for a California construction company. He belongs to a
diarists' network and has committed himself to posting an entry daily.
He has kept his word since January 2000, although his diary writing in
fact started in 1986. 'Live from New-York – Lisa's Journey'[6] is the
second diary under consideration. In this weblog, which she started at
the beginning of June 2001 after having kept a conventional diary on
and off all her life, Lisa, a thirty-six-year-old executive, delineates her
ongoing autobiographical narrative. Lisa belongs to a sado-masochist
diarists' webring, where sexually explicit entries are acceptable,
although these are by no means the sole purpose of her writing. As I
will attempt to show later on, the description of erotic scenes plays an
important if paradoxical part in her narrative of self. Both Lisa's and
Bunt Sign's voices are hauntingly distinctive and their diaries make
for captivating reading.

These writers, who use pseudonyms and might be expected to hide
behind the screen, in fact display a large number of photographs. Bunt
Sign puts up a complete photo album of his family (his parents, his
sister and two nephews), as well as a few photographs of himself as a
child, a youngster and as an adult. Lisa similarly includes a picture of
her late mother and several ones of herself at various ages. More
technologically oriented than Bunt Sign, she uses her digital camera
to experiment with self-portraits. Being taken with the camera held at
arm's length, the pictures are often imperfect through lack of proper
distance; shots taken from up close indeed tend to distort the features
of the subject being photographed. She nevertheless includes them in
her gallery as experiments in self-representation. Apart from these few
instances, however, prettiness is the rule in the portraits of the diarists
and of their families, an aesthetic choice encouraged by the
generalization of digital cameras which, by enabling the instant
evaluation of the pictures and removing the need for paper prints,
make it possible to get rid of any snapshot that fails to provide an
acceptable rendering of people, objects or places.

Both diarists place their self-portraits and the pictures of their
families in separate "photo albums" for Bunt Sign, or "galleries" for
Lisa, with a short caption serving as identification and in some cases
longer narratives of important family events. The iconic representation
does not stand on its own, but goes together with a text that, however,

---

[6]   http://www.section12.com/users/lisa_p/pictures/oldpage/bio.html Quotations from
this diary will be identified by the letters *LL* and the entry date. Although Lisa's diary
is now offline, excerpts can still be accessed thanks to the Wayback Machine,
http://web.archive.org/web/*/http://www.section12.com/users/lisa_p/.

gives precedence to iconicity while downplaying its own significance. Each one of the snapshots included in the collection abides by conventional rules of composition and coloring and this is especially true whenever the diarists attempt to photograph themselves. The writers are well aware of the precepts governing the genre of the self-portrait, and cast their countenance accordingly, for the most part looking straight at the camera, holding themselves erect and dignified, yet with an engaging expression (*LL* Jul. 8, 2002), thus demonstrating the lasting influence of the seventeenth century painters who established the rules of self-portraiture, and providing a further instance of the intertextuality governing diaristic and photographic practices.

In Bunt Sign's diary, the family pictures function as extensions of the traditional family album, providing a smooth, seamless narrative of family history. The iconicity of the pictures is supplemented with texts in which discord among family members or estrangement between them are only barely hinted at, without any detail being supplied (*BS*, Jan. 8, 2000). One of the stated reasons for such discretion is the need to protect the privacy of relatives (*BS*, Aug. 11, 2000). The other, unspoken reason may be that the author is constructing an image of self which has very little to do with self-knowledge or growth, and a great deal to do with a careful, socially acceptable reconstruction of times past – a family romance in its own right, one of whose purposes is to reinforce the construct of self put in place through diary-writing. His photo album presents his family as a collective with an identifiable and clearly delineated history, while his entries function in part as explorations of his position within that collective.

Lisa, on the other hand, hints at childhood abuse (*LL* Apr. 28, 2002), and alludes to an abusive former companion, without, however, dwelling on particulars (*LL* Apr. 5, 2002); she also includes accounts of her quarrels with her father (*LL* January 30, 2002, March 10, 2002). Yet her family romance is no less conventional. Her narrative fits into the contemporary confessional mode and partly matches the *topoi* of the woman as victim in a toxic family environment. But these dark elements are counterbalanced by the vibrant homage she pays to her dead mother (*LL* Jan. 11, 2002), whom she depicts as a model of kindness and altruism, in a text where her picture is embedded as in a shrine. The two narratives (the angelic mother and the hateful father), combined with her own longing for a stable love-affair point to a highly romanticized view of family life, which ultimately is not that remote from Bunt Sign's idealizations. Her iconography unites with her entries, both striving for the same goal.

For Bunt Sign as well as for Lisa, then, the prettiness of the pictures combined with the romanticization of the family narrative seem to point to the deep-set desire of the writers to reassure both themselves and readers about the serenity and sheer normalcy of their inner and outer landscapes. Both diarists studiously avoid going beyond the most obvious and trite kind of symbolism whenever linking text and pictures, so as to enmesh readers into the web of meaning they have created and preclude their probing beyond the surface (de Mijolla-Mellor 103). By imposing a narrative that guides and controls perception and interpretation, the pictures and their accompanying text therefore inevitably veil what they are purportedly revealing. Pictures can be seen as idealizing and therefore as distorting mirrors whose chief purpose is to cover up the void that is fundamentally at the heart of the subject.

Despite the blurring effect of representation, the presence of pictures raises the question of the privacy of these intimate writings: family members or acquaintances might easily stumble on these photo galleries and on the accompanying texts, which sometimes reveal thoughts or deeds that are generally expected to remain private. Therefore the voluminous "picture galleries" the diarists include perhaps bespeak an obscure, unspoken attempt at coming out (Lejeune 2000b: 423), at achieving a self-revelation which would allow them to make their private and public selves coincide and hence put an end to the tension inevitably deriving from concealing important aspects of one's personality. This is a distinct possibility for Lisa, whose sexual preferences lie outside the pale of convention, and who devotes much thought to the manner in which she discloses them to her partners. In Bunt Sign's case, however, 'coming out' is not linked to sexuality, as we shall see further on, but to the articulate, often witty personality apparent in his journal entries, yet hidden by a "tongue-tied and awkward" demeanor in his daily life (*BS* Jan. 23, 2000.) For both of them, revealing their secret truths is fraught with subversive potentialities.

Both writers probably also incur the risk of discovery because, by undertaking a diary, they commit themselves to truth telling: this is an essential part of the covenant entered into by diarists (Lejeune 1975). That 'truth' might be a construction when writing a diary is irrelevant at this point. What matters is that the galleries of portraits of the writers and of their families help to give substance and consistency to their own story and to their personal history. Portraits assure not only the readers, but primarily the writers, of the reality of their existence. In addition, and more importantly, they function as devices for self-reassurance when confronting the feelings of vacuity and nothingness arising from the realization that the passage of time annihilates much of what constitutes experience. Pictures supplement memory, and representations of corporeity in its temporal dimension rescue consciousness from the void, flesh it out and thus help re-member the disjointed past.

3.2. Physical and social background

Pictures of physical locations appear abundantly. Bunt Sign's entries always feature a landscape photograph, which might be either the view from his window, or a particular detail of his garden. Lisa displays numerous pictures of various houses and landscapes; both insert snapshots of their living-rooms or of their desks, kitchens, etc. As always, such pictures are commented on, however briefly, in a blend of textuality and iconicity which does little to dispel the basic opacity of pictures.

These perspectives on the writers' surroundings seem to function in two distinct ways. One of them is that they give the reader a sense of depth, as they contribute to ground the diary in physical reality; as such they also function as a kind of visual archive, offering the reader an inside look at middle-class life in America. Mentions of central air-conditioning (*LL* July 5, 2002) or descriptions of Tivo, the television recording service (*BS* Jan. 6, 2002), combined with snapshots of a family birthday party (*BS* June 11, 2000) or of a baseball game (*BS* Sept. 10, 2000, Sept. 11, 2002), to quote but a few examples, may be seen as primary sources of social history providing the basis for an ethnography of contemporary social mores in the United States. In addition, entries written after the 9/11 attacks by both Bunt Sign (*BS* Sept. 11, 2001 *seq.*) and Lisa (*LL* Sept. 12, 2001 *seq.*) as well as pictures of the World Trade Center and then of Ground Zero in the latter's weblog add to the archival function of these documents and illuminate the juncture of historical events and individual perception in diaristic writing online. Thus a different and important perspective on large-scale events may come into being and be confronted with the discourses of historians or authorities. Furthermore, in a serious crisis, "outside events […] become component parts of the crisis of the soul. […] Keeping a diary becomes an action that contributes to preserving the self, while defining its relationship with History" (Ball 2003: 104).[7] In other words, through the use of pictures, national and international current events intrude in private writings. The diary then offers a space that mediates between the diarist and the raw material of the news as provided by informational channels; it turns into a means of helping diarists to work through their own interpretations, enthusiasms or fears, as well as providing a highly individualized take on contemporary events. The pictures and texts in a diary may therefore fulfil a documentary, testimonial function.

The second function of these photographs is more inward-looking, for the representations of landscapes operate primarily as metonymies: far from being ornamental, the cloudy skies, the dramatic sunsets or the stormy weather, but also the pictures of flowers in bloom and of lush growths of wisteria all either reflect or contrast with the writers' states of mind. Bunt Sign more particularly uses his pictures of sunsets or of trees to lighten the predominantly somber mood of some entries (*BS* Feb. 5, 2001). His snapshots of the birds or cats straying into his garden provide a lighthearted counterpoint to the psychological difficulties he often labors under, thus fulfilling an important narrative function. His pictures combine the ephemerality of the snapshot with the repetitiveness of the content, in an odd tribute to the beauty of the instant – and faith in its repeatability.

3.3. Food

Food and its corollary, dieting, course throughout online diary writing (*BS* Jul. 13, 2000, Sept. 7, 2001; *LL* Jul. 27, 2002); recipes or pictures of memorable dishes frequently appear (*BS* Aug. 9, 2000); brand names of cereals, chocolate bars and other foods are also mentioned. Eating at restaurants is often described, most noticeably by Lisa, whose social life is more active than Bunt Sign's. Family meals of course figure prominently, as well as the sociability induced by diary-writing itself. The meals taken with other diarists met through the webring give rise to comments which are then linked to one another in the journals of each of the persons involved in the meeting. Food thus retains its traditional function of incorporating individuals into groups.

---

[7]   " Dans les grandes crises, les éléments extérieurs […] deviennent des éléments constitutifs de la crise de l'âme. […] La rédaction du journal devient un acte qui contribue à la préservation du moi, tout en le définissant dans ses rapports avec l'Histoire".

The dominant theme, however, is that of dieting. Bunt Sign interprets his craving for food as a displacement of his feelings of inadequacy and of his mild social phobia. Lisa establishes a direct link between her unhappiness and her lapse from thinness and fitness and compares her craving for food to an 'addiction' (*LL* Apr. 13, 2002). She mentions undergoing therapy and describes attending 'recovery meetings' for her 'eating disorder' (*LL* Apr. 19, 2002). For both of them, the struggle never ceases: "So the third day into my [...] diet, Grady brings me a piece of the chocolate birthday cake from his party [...]. Did I eat the cake? Naturally. I'm a weak, weak person" (*BS* Jan. 23, 2000). Lisa's diary features a special section entitled 'Progress Notes' entirely devoted to dieting and working out and carefully recording weight gain or loss (*LL* Dec. 27, 2001 *seq.*)

Growing fat and slimming down become stages in the narratives of self and the fastidious descriptions of their struggle with the temptation of fattening foods, repetitive and trivial as they are, turn into stages in a Sisyphean progression towards an imaginary state of goodness. Dieting can indeed be linked to the religious ascetic practises common in earlier periods, when fasting or abstaining from appetizing foods were part and parcel of religious observance. But as will become obvious as this analysis develops, dieting is one of the ways in which the diarists try to address and control the unruliness of the body – an unruliness which is inherent in corporeity.

3.4. The body proper

The diarists themselves are of course the main focus of these self-representational works. Because the body is an interface between the inner world of each person and the outside world, it is at the same time silent, nearly undecipherable and the instigator of language, of streams of words mediating the relationship of each subject to their body and to the world at large. But the body is also an interface between each individual's inner life and others; the body is what enables each individual to conceive of themselves as unique and to interact with others; as such, the body also mediates the relationship between the private and the public, the personal and the social realms. The perception of the body's unicity is offset by the experience of its multiplicity, as the various inscriptions of others and of society both on and in the body turn it into a buffer zone, constantly shaped by conflicting inner and outer forces. This tension between unicity and duality or multiplicity is apparent in Bunt Sign's and Lisa's diaries.

Bunt Sign hardly seems to do more than skim the surface of his life throughout his diary. Both his pictures and his writings are governed by a sense of decorum: never is there any unconventional exposure of any aspect of his inner life; romance or sex are conspicuously absent from either text or images. However, an oddly revealing narrative does emerge, for all that it abides by the most rigorous decency laws.

It is first and foremost the narrative of a suffering body, with descriptions of a tooth ache (*BS* Aug. 8, 2000), or of his back acting up (*BS*, Sept.1, 2000). In a striking episode (*BS* July 11, 2000), Bunt Sign feels a lump in his throat which keeps him from speaking, yet fails to call his HMO for an appointment, because of his stated reluctance to be in touch with other people apart from his immediate family. When recounting his latest holidays, just below a family picture displaying a child whose birthday is being celebrated, he mentions his "nosebleeds" (*BS* July 19, 2002).

A process of metaphoric displacement and substitution seems to be at work here: his body seems to be the only possible transmitter of a message, for lack of words to talk about body matters. Language can inscribe inner conflicts, feelings and emotions into the shared discursive space of intersubjectivity. But Bunt Sign paradoxically seems to be in a situation in which conflicts or emotions cannot gain access to this discursive space: language – which he uses with talent when writing journal entries – seems to collapse whenever his inner conflicts threaten to emerge. In a bout of self-examination and self-deprecatory irony, Bunt Sign thus writes (*BS* Aug.29, 2002):

> In the same spirit that I never drive without the radio on so that I won't hear anything in the car engine that I don't want to hear, I work all day with either the TV on or music playing. I don't pay all that much attention to either when I'm concentrating on a task, but it's good to have it there for when my concentration lapses and I might accidentally let a bad thought creep into my head. (…)
>
> If the thoughts I've been expressing here lately seem a little superficial and disjointed, it's because I'm not letting myself wallow too deeply in anything that might be troubling or might wrench me in some disturbing direction. Until now, of course, which is where all this is coming from.
>
> And I'm not about to let this go on long enough to let the darkness take over, or to bring any demons to light. I'm not even going to repair that mangled metaphor, because I kind of like the paradoxical nature of it.

In this passage, Bunt Sign shows he is perfectly aware of the fact that his diary is "a linguistic space that conceals – and tries to seal itself against – the gap of the unconscious" (Benstock 1988: 29). Describing his strategies to evade disturbing thoughts, he still refuses to tell his readers what these thought are about. Yet what he cannot convey or refuses to convey through language comes through as a gesture, a kind of violent, physical acting out. In Freudian terms, his body becomes a site of symptoms. In entry after entry, through its postures, its attitudes, its reactions to minor stimuli, his body overtakes him, bypasses the repressive hold he maintains on language and gives expression to what he wants to hide. States of mind are thus communicated through ailments, which give a visible bodily inscription to hidden processes.

Bunt Sign takes stock of these ailments in a process of narration whose purpose is twofold. It is first of all illocutionary, i.e. narrating the disorder is an action unto itself which may be interpreted in a variety of ways by the readers. The illocutionary act of relating perplexing pains and aches moves the self-representational narrative along and enables readers to become aware of the presence of troubling undercurrents beneath the stolidly conventional surface of the diarist's narrative (Elam 1990: 163-164). But narration is also a re-enactment through language and as such it creates the discursive space necessary to distance the narrator from his own experience. The online diary functions as a writing space in which these physical traces can be both acknowledged and left behind. This is necessary because pain turns the body into the Other, unpredictable and threatening, and hence endangers his sense of self. Bunt Sign therefore uses his diaristic narrative as a distance-producing device in an attempt to gain control over the otherness exposed by the advent of pain.

Pain plays a different though no less essential part in Lisa's weblog. Firstly, just like Bunt Sign, she mentions her ailments, giving for instance a full account of her fears when undergoing gynaecological tests (*LL* May 14, 2002) and showing her body in a clinical light (Berthelot 1997: 67). But unlike her male counterpart, for whom sex is a glaring absence, Lisa combines descriptions of her daily routines and states of mind with an erotic diary, encompassing descriptions of what she calls 'scenes' as well as her search for a stable relationship. Her body therefore might be expected to be a site not of symptoms, as for Bunt Sign, but of pleasure. This expectation, however, is constantly thwarted by her choice of sexual behavior. In the few but graphic descriptions she provides of the mistreatments she craves and submits to (*LL* Aug. 27, 2001 *seq.*), pleasure is only a side-effect. As she describes her 'training' and defines the degrees of pain she wants to experience and the various implements used by her partner, the suffering body she describes becomes a pathway to selfhood through control.

As theorized by psycho-analyst Didier Anzieu, for the masochist, "the function of individuation of the Self can only be achieved through physical suffering (tortures) and moral suffering (humiliations)" (Anzieu 1985: 133).[8] Lisa internalises a set of rules which are literally inscribed in her body (Foucault 1975: 32-35) by the contract she draws up with her partner stipulating what kind and degree of pain will be inflicted. Even though appearing to submit, she is in fact in total command of her own body; she appropriates it by setting up and enacting her own law and in so doing, she exercises control over its otherness, as well as over her supposed tormentor. That submission and domination belong in the same sphere is perceived by the diarist herself, who writes: "In my heart of hearts, I don't believe a Master exists for me. Could I ever have that level of respect for a man?" (*LL* May 31, 2001). In the relationships she describes, she is very much the prescriber of behavior (*LL* May 10, 2002), further underscoring the subtle and complex links woven between submission and domination.

Freud and later on Lacan have theorized the masochistic position as one of attempted mastery over the primary oppositions between *good* and *bad*, making it possible to fuse the two categories into one. The eroticization of pain, by denying the split between pleasure and pain, is thus a way of achieving control over the split within the subject. Masochists attempt to inscribe on their body all kinds of cuts, nicks, incisions, wounds and burns with a wide variety of implements, usually in a highly theatricalized fashion, obvious in the case of online diaries in the lengthy descriptions and sometimes gruesome pictures of such scenes. In so doing, they are reproducing on their own flesh the original split all human beings undergo in the early stages of their development. This split is the necessary condition for the existence of language. For masochists, the cuts and wounds inflicted on their body become literal transliterations of the symbolic split within the speaking subject; by appropriating control over the mistreatments they subject their body to, masochists do their utmost to deny and hence achieve mastery over that primary split. In addition, the infringement

---

[8] "La fonction d'individuation du Soi ne trouve à s'accomplir que dans la souffrance physique (les tortures) et morale (les humiliations)".

on the Other's body carried out in such scenes is a paradoxical attempt to merge with the other by denying the essential separation of humans (Rey-Flaud 2002: 84-86).

Writing about the *jouissance* caused by the suffering she submits to, Lisa dominates at the same time the division within the self, the separation from the Other and the symbolic categories of language. Both Lisa's writing and her use of pain in carefully controlled situations function in similar ways, as devices to keep in check the uncontrollable in corporeity – and thus attain a sense of selfhood.

This is why the apparent divergences between the representations of corporeity in the two diaries under consideration in fact cover up many underlying similarities. For Bunt Sign, it seems that corporeity can be addressed in his text only through socially acceptable channels: pain, food, dieting, bingeing, etc. His own relationship with body matters apparently under-emphasizes corporeity and is carefully swathed in conventional, culturally familiar channels, at a total remove from formless outpourings. For Lisa, alternating descriptions of her melancholic moods with those of her longing for love and a few erotic scenes, corporeity seems to be in the foreground. In fact, Lisa's diary, brutally candid as it may seem, is basically similar to Bunt Sign's apparent lack of regard for the body. Both use their suffering bodies and their writing up of their experience of corporeity in order to integrate the discontinuous fragments of their identities, finally taking possession of their body through representation.

For both diarists, moreover, the self-portraits and the pictures of various physical locations combine with the daily entries to tame the *unheimlich,* the feeling of strangeness that overcomes individuals as they realize that the Other is within themselves – not least because the body, familiar as it is, ultimately manages to escape control. One of the ways of coming to terms with the strangeness within is, as we have seen, a focus on corporeity and on its perception. Embodied writing in online self-representational writing is thus first and foremost a way for diarists to "incur the risk of experiencing [their] body, of discovering the very flesh of [their] existence" (Sibony 1995: 285).[9] This is why Bunt Sign's outwardly utterly conventional approach of the body nevertheless is a way of hacking up an opening in a situation where the body seems to be negated, in the process giving himself some purchase towards coming to terms with corporeity. When his body asserts itself despite his best efforts at repression and denial, the

---

9   "Il prend [...] le risque d'exister comme corps, de découvrir la chair même de son existence".

ensuing confrontation is an ever so slight movement towards self-awareness. Lisa's masochistic testing of the boundaries of pain can similarly be seen as a persistent quest for a unified self through both control of corporeity and embodied writing.

The passageway or transitional space afforded by the diary allows the writers to institute the body as language and to embody language, in a back-and-forth, mirror-like movement, and hence to initiate an identity formation or re-formation process grounded in corporeity. Body and identity thus constitute and institute each other. By retracing each day's stream of trivial, mundane events and anchoring them in corporeity, both Bunt Sign and Lisa turn their bodies into a theater of the self. In so doing, they turn their lives into a relatively ordered narrative and produce themselves as subjects. The construct they build shifts away from post-modernist conceptions of multiple selves or fragmented authorship in an attempt to re-institute the unified, embodied subject of traditional narratives. That the attempt is doomed to fail is irrelevant inasmuch as the complex interplay of textual and graphic representations of corporeity contains, in and of itself, both the means and the end of self-representational writing, where process is all.

4. Gendered self-representation ?

4.1. Fluid bodies

Gender can be briefly defined as the social construction of sexual differences. This point has to be made because the notion of gender has tended to lose its definition as a construct and to be naturalized or biologized (Butler 1990: 147). Social representations of masculinity and femininity too often tend to be viewed as innate or ontological in nature, ending up in a stereotypical vision of a-historical feminine or masculine   specificities, at the expense of individualities, and reinforcing the oldest and the worst clichés about men and women even while purporting to defend the latter.

What is indeed abundantly clear from the observation of a large number of diaries, as well as from the observation of the two diaries under consideration here, is that embodied identities in online diaries seem to blur conventional gender lines; fluidity in self-definition appears to be the norm for both men and women, who use identical strategies to create and consolidate their fictional personae. For instance, it is impossible to cast Lisa into the role of the feminine Other (Anderson 2001: 102) to any man, least of all Bunt Sign, because both diarists are equally preoccupied with their own sense of otherness in relation to themselves, their self-perception and their social selves. What is more, the most stereotypically feminine subjects, such as being in love, cooking, dieting, cleaning house, maintaining relationships with friends and family appear just as consistently in Bunt Sign's and Lisa's diaries. The same holds true for work- and politics-related issues, i.e. the public sphere, traditionally ascribed to men: both diarists describe their work at length, although Bunt Sign tends to discuss politics at more frequent intervals. These two writers, stark opposites in everything from their geographical locations to their jobs to their families – and also, of course, in the matter of sexuality – share in fact a preoccupation with corporeity in all its guises. Both the male and the female bodies shown in their diaries are the objects of representation through text and images, both the male and female subjects are producers and consumers of representations of corporeity. Gender therefore is not a useful category when looking at identity construction in online diaries. It can indeed hardly be used in a context in which the major goal is construction of self, with its attendant focus on individual choice subverting cultural conventions and dominant cultural narratives.

What can be found, on the other hand, is the record of individual struggles with gender definition, a process congruent with that of identity construction. Several online diarists document their efforts to push back the boundaries of gender, and to make their bodies coincide with their self-perception. Columbine and Shmuel will be two cases in point.

4.2. Columbine

Columbine's site has gone through several versions over the years. In its first version, the drawing on the front page of his journal is that of a romantic feminine face on a background of lush vegetation.[10] Although Columbine's journal has been moved and has diversified into a journal, a weblog and fiction writings, each with their own URL, his original site still gives access to his journal archives and his pictorial autobiography.[11] His self-revelation occurs in gradual stages, using a mixture of drawings, text and pictures.

---

[10] Alewife's Bayou, http://www.inu.org/alewife/index.htm
[11] http://www.inu.org/pihua/archives.htm

In his nine page biographical sketch,[12] the writer carefully maintains an ambiguity regarding his gender. He does so by writing about himself in the third person , and by using androgynous pseudonyms: Columbine may be used for a man or a woman, and the first page describes Columbine as a woman, the second one as a "boygirl" and the third page provides the drawing of a naked woman to illustrate a brief textual self-portrait:

> Columbine is a skinny woman with very long limbs. She has small breasts, thick messy hair that tangles itself spontaneously and defies all attempts to style it. She hates her feet (large), her nose (unattractively shaped), her hands (they look hard-used), and her height (too tall). But, because her figure is so atypical for a woman, she can actually wear most of the ridiculous clothing that the stores claim is sized for females.[13]

It is only upon reaching page four that Columbine reveals his gender, pretending to do so under duress: "You really are going to force me to say it, aren't you? Oh, all right. Columbine isn't actually female. But not by choice. When I began this journal, my gender dysphoria was one of its main themes. It isn't anymore. Life is stabler now". The text is placed next to a photograph which closely follows the conventions of the self-portrait with mirror put in place by seventeenth century painters. We can see him holding the camera and preparing to snap the picture. Columbine's gaze is level and focused and bears witness to the high seriousness of his questioning.[14] The intertextuality inherent in the use of the hallowed form of self-portraiture points to the fact that the portrait is the reflection, not of a specific person only, but of a mesh of intertwined reflections pointing to the relationship between the collective and the individual. The portrait thus reflects the individual's uniqueness even as it is inscribed in a system of social representations. Columbine's self-portrait is no stranger to this and seems to reach a compromise between the social reality of his masculine body and the inner reality of his questionings about gender.

The next page of Columbine's autobiographical sketch reverts to drawing, with the picture of an imaginary plant character which used to be his avatar in online games. The text located next to the drawing emphasizes the issue of gender online: "[Some] went crazy trying to

---

[12]   http://www.inu.org/pihua/bio.htm
[13]   http://www.inu.org/pihua/bio3.htm
[14]   http://www.inu.org/pihua/bio4.htm

give it a gender. "You've got to be one or the other". They had no problems with the plant aspect, but were unable to comprehend interacting with a neuter creature".[15] The next photograph shows him to be dressed in full feminine gear, while the next one is of his face, bathed in light, alongside one brief line of text, asserting that "Columbine is occasionally a transcendent mental experience".[16] The final two pictures are a close-up portrait in black and white, showing Columbine to be a man with fine features and long hair. The pictures themselves correspond to the most conventional codes of 'beauty': the lighting is soft, the model is demurely looking at the camera, the background is almost invisible. The model seems to stand in nowhere land, perhaps involuntarily giving away the symbolic positioning of a person who refuses to stand firmly within a single gender, but attempts to straddle both.

This pictorial autobiography indeed tries to show that the body is not merely a given, but a system of social signs on which one can inscribe a personal mark. Because Columbine's pictures foreground the constructed character of gender codes, they also foreground the basic manipulability of such codes. Columbine seeks to use his pictures as rhetorical constructions, instruments for self-reinvention liable to assault gender codes and de-essentialize them. The body becomes the locus of self-knowledge, or at least self-exploration. But this locus needs to be constituted by the gaze of others, hence the photographs and their public nature.

Columbine, then, rebels against the identification of body and self, and militates for the right to have a degree of choice; he manipulates his image as a way of manipulating his body. It is however interesting to note that while modifying his appearance, what Columbine seems to strive for and get, is a feminization of his image that conforms with the most commonplace stereotypes of femininity: softness, regular features, a sweet countenance. The body in its materiality is toned down, euphemized. The illusion of gender change Columbine tries to set up finally ends ups in a conventionalized representation of femininity, fetishizing the erotic, gender-coded attributes of the feminine, which can therefore hardly be interpreted as an ironic take on femininity or on social inscriptions of gender. Even while trying to reconceptualize and reconfigure his gendered body, Columbine knows full well that he cannot escape the coding mechanism and the gender stereotyping that goes with them. His role-playing is not a

---

[15]   http://www.inu.org/pihua/bio5.htm
[16]   http://www.inu.org/pihua/bio7.htm

deconstruction weapon but a mirror for his ambivalence and for his subjectivity, never shown engaging his desires or acting upon them, thus remaining a liminal experiment in gender identity. Columbine's pictorial autobiographical sketch, while trying to address the issue of the boundaries of each gender, is ultimately defeated by the external cultural discourses regarding femininity and eventually participates in their production and reproduction. Shaking off gender stereotypes turns out to be a near-impossible feat, perhaps because of the use of pictures which, by reducing discourse to culture-specific stereotypes, somewhat reduce complexity and semiotic thickness. The attempt itself may, however, be the whole point.

4.3. Shmuel

Shmuel's case is far different because the changes recorded in his journal do not take place in the realm of the symbolic only, but have a bearing in real life. His journal was started in 1999, while he was an English student at Queens College.[17] We learn he is an aspiring writer and his texts indeed evince unmistakable talent. What slowly becomes apparent is that Shmuel is uncomfortable within his religion, his body, his studies, and his job as an instructor to undergraduate students. His diary is a humorous, often highly comical chronicle of his efforts at figuring himself out, written in a distinctive, deceptively straightforward style.

As his diaristic narrative unfolds, we learn that he has begun to feel constricted by the very strict variant of Judaism his family adheres to. His general unease with himself and his life leads to a severe case of writer's block and causes him to postpone completing his master's degree by a semester. This moral and spiritual crisis is accompanied by a process of transformation of his appearance, since this is the moment he chooses to shave his beard, the major bodily sign of his belonging to a specific religious group. He refrains from elaborating on his decision, but he does explain the religious repercussions of his course of action:

> I need to get back to that homework, but I know I owe you
> guys a long and detailed explanation. The short version, for
> the moment: no, I haven't abandoned Orthodox Judaism, nor

---

[17] *Shmuel's Soapbox, op.cit.* All subsequent entries will be identified within the text, between brackets, by the date only.

am I really considering doing so at the moment. I *am* abandoning the customs of a particular subgroup within Orthodox Judaism, a subgroup to which my father has belonged since he was 17 or so, and a subgroup with which I haven't agreed ideologically pretty much as long as I've had an ideology to call my own. There are plenty of Orthodox Jews who shave; that particular subgroup doesn't.

The one teensy little catch -- which has held me back from doing anything of the sort until now -- is that I don't have any particular group or rabbi to switch my allegiance over to. I've decided to stop waiting until that happens, which may be the one major infraction I *am* committing just now, but I seem to be holding the line at that. (February 11, 2002 entry. Emphasis in the text).

The context is implicitly that of the rift between Shmuel and his father, a rift which is alluded to but never explained in full (February 22, 2002 and May 19, 2002 entries); Shmuel is nevertheless well aware of the fact that his decision leaves him in a religious limbo, and of the fact that he is breaking a rule as a way of breaking with his father. Yet, when providing a before/after photograph, with some approving comments on his appearance, Shmuel entirely leaves out the religious significance of his shaving his beard (February 21, 2002). The reader indeed gradually discovers that this is only the first step in a far-reaching process of self-transformation in which religion does not necessarily play the lead part (June 2, 2002).

Later developments indicate a playful tinkering with gender codes: "I don't care for body hair, even though I come naturally loaded with the stuff. So I'm experimenting a bit. I'd gotten a disposable razor in a free sample pack way back in September... as of earlier today, it's one leg down, and one to go. If nothing else, I figure I've gotta [sic] even them out now" (June 10, 2002). The following entries are just as light in tone; Shmuel obviously maintains the continuity of his humorous style throughout, even when addressing the issue of gender roles, and the blur in the boundaries of his sexual identity due to his experimentation (July 31, 2002). Trying out new behaviors continues with a visit to a Times Square strip club in New-York, leading him to reflect on his increased willingness to leave religious observance behind (March 3, 2003). The whole process of physical and spiritual self-transformation is one that has been recorded in and helped along by the journal he has been keeping.

What Shmuel seems to have been trying hard to do is to escape the rigidity of the binary, either/or difference between the sexes, not only through language or pictures, i.e. through representation, but also through modifications in his body. Repeatedly saying that he is not inclined towards homosexuality, he still wants to experiment with some of the trappings of femininity, thus attempting to undo the knot of identity, sexual organs and discourse. Using his writings to explore feminine practises, Shmuel is engaged in a search for a deeper understanding of gender difference as it was imposed by culture on his body. In Lacanian terms, "the imposition of gender difference on infants – culture imposed on nature – gives rise to identity as a problematic. [...] Yet, both males and females are effects of the phallic signifier, itself the effect of difference" (Ragland-Sullivan 1991: 62). Shmuel's journal writing forces upon him the realization that gender identity is first and foremost a fiction, built "on the quicksand of a void" (Ragland-Sullivan 1991: 63). The language of self-representation thus ultimately deconstructs the "illusion of Oneness" (Ragland-Sullivan 1991: 65) and underscores the fundamental multiplicity of being, while simultaneously offering an overview of times past that, in and of itself, creates a narrative. The diarist's body, mediated by the language of self-representation, thus becomes the locus for the exploration of that multiplicity and of that narrativity. In the process, language gives Shmuel some access to his own, now apparently unveiled desire. However, "the major function of language is not to find answers, communicate, or provide information, but to project narcissism, protect egos, mask *jouissance*, negotiate desire. Dreams, literary texts, sexual relations, analysis, pleasure, pain, symptoms, repetition, the feminine and religion all reside on the slope of fading, gaps and questions. It is not closure or solutions that mark these phenomena, but mystery and enigma" (Ragland-Sullivan 1991: 69). Decoding that ceaselessly re-forming enigma is at the heart of Shmuel's explorations of gender identity.

5. Online embodiment

As this chapter draws to its close, the fears regarding corporeity raised by the advent of the computer and of Internet-mediated communication can now be addressed. The written word on the Internet rests by definition on an absence generated by writing: the apparent absence of a body and of a voice, made invisible and inaudible by the technological apparatus. Yet authors and critics alike can testify to the highly physical approach writing entails. For some, "the act of writing is as wrenching as sex and necessarily involves the body" (Laporte 1973: 129).[18] For Roland Barthes, "writing involves the hand, hence writing *is* the body, its drives, its controls, its rhythms, its ponderousness, its shifts, its complications, its escapes, in short, [...] [writing reflects] subjects weighed down with their desire and their unconscious" (Barthes 1981: 184).[19] The involvement of the body online is highlighted by the evolution of online texts themselves. As computer and Internet users know from experience, dragging the mouse across the screen is a precise physical gesture; moreover, whenever the mouse approaches a hyperlink, the cursor turns into the image of a hand, suggesting our hand's actual pressure on some kind of switch (Mabillot 2002). As a result, exploring a page mixes both the visual and the tactile perception of text. The written sign verges towards the material object, requiring a physical action. The body therefore is undeniably present, even when it seems totally mediated by the surface of the screen, because it is required to interact with the online text, in a process that merges the realms of the physical and of the abstract. Either dragging the mouse across the screen or working the aptly named touch-pad of a laptop underscore the part played by the senses in the readers' search for significance.

Furthermore, the body is necessarily part and parcel of online experience, for diarists or for their readers, because it is always produced and construed discursively: there is no such thing as a material body separated from language. Reading diaries or writing them online therefore means connecting with embodied experience and inventing an approach of reality in which body surfaces reflect the depths of selfhood, and writing embodies the self. Nowhere is this more evident than in erotic writing, where text strives for the palpability and for the expressiveness of flesh.

In addition, for all the talk of virtuality and immateriality, language itself is far from being either abstract or disembodied, as linguistic theory and psychoanalysis have evidenced. Lacan indeed underscores that language is not immaterial: "it is a subtle body, but a body. Words are trapped in all the corporeal images which captivate the subject" (Lacan 1966: 301). In other words, the signifier itself, viewed in its materiality, is inseparable from meaning. The body of the signifier-phonemes, of morphemes, is indissolubly linked with the infinite of the signified and resonates in and with the body of the speaking

---

[18] "Au contraire, l'acte d'écrire, aussi déchirant que le sexuel, passe par le corps".
[19] "L'écriture , c'est la main, c'est donc le corps: ses pulsions, ses contrôles, ses rythmes, ses pesées, ses glissements, ses complications, ses fuites, bref [...] [l'écrit reflète] le sujet lesté de son désir et de son inconscient".

subject. Writing itself "becomes a body which carries words, not towards someone else, but towards other parts of oneself" (Sibony 1995: 276). Online embodied writing thus becomes a fully rounded, thorough representation of corporeity channelling a necessarily self-defeating quest for a unified self.

Conclusion

There is a major difference between contemporary diary readers and the audience of, say, Plutarch's *Parallel Lives*. The latter looked for a normative, prescriptive narrative, liable to serve as the foundation for their own lives. Modelling one's life after that of a great man was indeed a recurrent motif in the Classical era; superior individuals were supposed to be able to enlighten and inspire run-of-the mill mortals and guide them through the meanderings of their lives.

The post-modern contemporary era, by contrast, provides not one, but a multiplicity of models, whose emergence is ascribed to diverse sources. For some, the rise of absolutism combined with the evolution of religious practises created the space required for the concept of the individual to emerge.[1] For others, the rise of democracy was key to the development of individualism. Tocqueville's 1835 description of democratic processes in America rests on just such an assumption:

> I can see teeming crowds of similar and equal people who ceaselessly pursue the small and vulgar pleasures they fill up their soul with. Each one of them, living apart, is as it were a stranger to the fate of all others: for him, his children and his particular friends form the entire human species; as to the remainder of his compatriots, he lives next to them, but he does not see them, he neither touches them nor feels them; he only exists in and for himself and, though he may still have a family, he may nonetheless be said to no longer have a homeland. (de Tocqueville 1840: 434)[2]

---

[1] See p. 4-6 *supra*.

[2] "Je vois une foule innombrable d'hommes semblables et égaux qui tournent sans repos sur eux-mêmes pour se procurer de petits et vulgaires plaisirs dont ils emplissent leur âme. Chacun d'eux, retiré à l'écart, est comme étranger à la destinée de tous les autres: ses enfants et ses amis particuliers forment pour lui toute l'espèce humaine; quant au demeurant de ses concitoyens, il est à côté d'eux, mais il ne les

From this point of view, democracy creates the conditions for a withdrawal into the private realm and thus instigates the mechanisms that unravel the social fabric and end up in promoting disinterest in civic life and individualism. As a consequence, the individual is supposedly reduced to his own resources to create behavior standards, in a drive towards an ideal type of autonomous individual which, for Durkheim, was one of the characteristics of modernity.

This view is further elaborated by Norbert Elias who, analyzing individualization processes over very long periods of time, points out that they are the end results of historical evolutions: "individuals free themselves [...] from the communities pre-ordained by their birth or from protective groups, and they have more freedom of choice. They may choose their fate with far more freedom. But then, they *must* choose their fate. Not only do they have the chance of becoming more autonomous, but they have to be so" (Elias 1991: 169).[3] If the social and political order which used to assign each individual a clearly defined, practically unchangeable position tends to crumble, then social success rests on the individual alone, whose responsibility thus becomes overwhelming. As pointed out by Alain Ehrenberg, who writes from Elias's perspective, "in our new normative configuration, individuals [...] must ground their behaviors in themselves: [...] symbolical landmarks are no longer a given. We have reached adulthood, meaning that we are responsible for ourselves to an extent that has never been equalled in the history of modern societies. This increased responsibility necessarily makes us more vulnerable, because it presupposes each individual's capacity to base their actions on their own private authority and personal judgement" (Ehrenberg 1995: 23).[4]

---

voit pas; il les touche et il ne les sent point; il n'existe qu'en lui-même et pour lui seul et, s'il lui reste encore une famille, on peut dire du moins qu'il n'a plus de patrie".

[3] "Les individus se dégagent [...] des communautés préétablies de naissance ou des groupes protecteurs. Et ils disposent d'une plus large liberté de choix. Ils peuvent bien plus librement décider de leur sort. Mais aussi *doivent-ils* décider de leur sort. Non seulement ils *peuvent* devenir plus autonomes, mais ils le doivent ". Italics in the text.

[4] "Dans notre nouvelle configuration normative, chacun [...] doit arrimer sa conduite sur lui-même: [...] les repères symboliques ne sont plus donnés par avance. Nous avons atteint l'âge d'homme, ce qui signifie que nous sommes responsables de nous-mêmes à un point jamais égalé dans l'histoire des sociétés modernes. Cette augmentation de la responsabilité nous rend, dans son mouvement même, plus vulnérables, car elle suppose la capacité de chacun à agir à partir de son autorité privée et de son jugement personnel ".

Nowhere is this truer than in America, where Transcendentalists built their philosophy on this very foundation – the individual as the benchmark for value. The phenomenal increase in individual freedom entailed by such a worldview goes together with an increase in the burden of responsibility each subject has to take on. This is where self-representational writing may fulfil a specific function for its readers, as an aid to form individual judgment about day-to-day behavior. Reading such texts is a way of finding out how others fashion their lives, and of comparing the solutions others have found with personal ones. The publicity given to other people's lives serves as a mirror onto which readers project their own questionings about behavior. While contemporary online diaries have no prescriptive or normative ambition, they *de facto* offer exemplars of social mores, and hence may contribute to alleviating the anxiety of inventing one's life as it is being lived.

As for the diarists themselves, publishing their innermost feelings on the Internet indeed increases vulnerability, but it also gives material existence, through writing, to an interiority that might otherwise have remained untapped. Diaristic writing on the Internet provides the added bonus of an audience which may and often does turn into an informal fellowship of like-minded people. Such a fellowship, limited as it is, nevertheless supplies the mirror the diarists need in order to construct an awareness of themselves as endlessly intricate beings. But the veil of language remains entire, obscuring new areas even as others begin to make sense and expressing with its inherent polysemy the ambivalence and complexity of the inner life of individuals. The mirror and the veil are the two inescapable facets of the experience of online writing.

Bibliography

1. Works cited

Adler, Patricia A. and Adler, Peter. 1994. 'Observational techniques' in Denzin, Norman and Lincoln, Yvonna S. (eds). *Handbook of Qualitative Research*. Newbury Park: Sage: 377-392.

Alterman, Eric. 2003. 'Determining the Value of Blogs' in *Nieman Report*. 57 (3) 85. http://www.nieman.harvard.edu/reports/03-3NRfall/V57N3.pdf. (Accessed October 2003).

Anderson, Linda. 2001. *Autobiography*. London: Routledge.

Anzieu, Didier. 1985; rpt. 1995. *Le moi-peau*. Paris: Dunod.

Assoun, Paul-Laurent. 1994. 'Freud et le rire' in A. W. Szafran et A. Nysenholc (eds) *Freud et le rire*. Paris: Métailié: 29-57.

--. 1995. 'Le for intérieur à l'épreuve de la psychanalyse: casuistique et inconscient' in *Le for intérieur*. Paris: PUF: 27-51.

Asimov, Isaac. *The Caves of Steel*. 1954; rpt. 1986. London: Grafton Books.

Bachelard, Gaston. 1938; rpt. 1970. *La formation de l'esprit scientifique*. Paris: Vrin.

Bakhtine, Mikhail. 1970. *La poétique de Dostoïevski*. (tr. I. Kolitcheff) (Collection Pierres Vives). Paris: Seuil.

Ball, David. 2003. 'L'intime et l'histoire: deux journaux personnels sous l'Occupation' in *Raison Présente*. 145: 103-126.

Barlow, John Perry. 1996. *A Cyberspace Independence Declaration*. Electronic Frontier Foundation. http://www.eff.org//Publications/John_Perry_Barlow/barlow_0296.declaration. (Accessed March 2002).

Roland Barthes. 1953; rpt. 1972. *Le degré zéro de l'écriture*. Paris: Seuil.

--. 1981. *Le grain de la voix: Entretiens 1962-1980*. Paris: Seuil.

Bays, Hillary. 2000. 'La politesse sur Internet: le don des objets imaginaires' in Wauthion, M., Simon, A.C. (eds). *Politesse et idéologie: rencontres de pragmatique et de rhétorique conversationnelles.* Louvain-La-Neuve: Peeters: 169-183.

Benedikt, Michael L. ed. 1991. *Cyberspace: First Steps.* Cambridge, MA: MIT Press.

Benstock, Shari (ed.). 1988. *The Private Self: Theory and Practice of Women's Autobiographical Writings.* Chapel Hill, N.C.: The University of North Carolina Press.

Bergeret, Jean. 1973. 'Pour une métapsychologie de l'humour' in *Revue française de psychanalyse* 4: 539-565.

Berners-Lee, Tim. 1992. 'What's New in 1992' in *History of Hypertext.* http://www.w3.org/History/19921103hypertext/hypertext/WWW/News/9201.html. (Accessed December 2001).

Berthelot, Francis. 1997. *Le corps du héros: pour une sémiologie de l'incarnation romanesque.* Paris: Nathan.

Blood, Rebecca. 2000. 'Weblogs: A History and a Perspective'. http://www.rebeccablood.net/essays/weblog_history.html . (Accessed February 2002).

Bloom, Harold. 1984. 'Mr. America'. *New-York Review of Books* (22 November 1984) 19-20.

Bloom, Lynn Z. 1996. 'I Write for Myself and Strangers' in Bunkers, Suzanne L., Huff, Cynthia A. (eds). *Inscribing the Daily: Critical Essays on Women's Diaries.* Amherst: University of Massachusetts Press.

Boelhower, William. 1991. 'The Making of Ethnic Autobiography in the United States' in Eakin, John Paul (ed.) *American Autobiography: Retrospect and Prospect.* Madison: The University of Wisconsin Press: 123-141.

Brohm, Jean-Marie. 1988. 'Corpus Symbolicum' in *Quel Corps?* 34/35: 22-40.

Bunkers, Suzanne L., Huff, Cynthia A. (eds). 1996. *Inscribing the Daily: Critical Essays on Women's Diaries.* Amherst: University of Massachusetts Press.

Butler, Judith. 1990. *Gender Trouble: Feminism and the Subversion of Identity.* New York: Routledge.

Carter, Angela. 1978. *The Sadeian Woman and the Ideology of Pornography.* New-York: Pantheon Books.

Chanfrault-Duchet, Marie-Françoise. 2000. 'Textualization of the Self and Gender-Identity in the Life-Story' in Cosslett, Tess, Lury, Celia, Summerfield, Penny (eds). *Feminism and Autobiography: Texts, Theories, Methods.* London: Routledge: 61-75.

Chanter, Tina. 1998. 'Postmodern subjectivity' in Alison M. Jaggar, Iris Marion Young (eds). *A Companion to Feminist Philosophy.* Oxford: Blackwell: 263-271.

Cosnier, Jacqueline. 1973. 'Humour et narcissisme' in *Revue française de psychanalyse* 4: 571-580.

Cosslett, Tess, Lury, Celia, Summerfield, Penny (eds.). 2000. *Feminism and Autobiography: Texts, Theories, Methods.* London: Routledge.

Debray, Régis . 1992. *Vie et mort de l'image: une histoire du regard en Occident.* Paris: Gallimard.

Dethurens, Pascal. 2000. 'Le héros cérébral et son corps' in Emmanuel Jacquart (ed.) *Le corps.* Special issue of *Vives Lettres.* 9: 97-108.

Domenach, Elise. 2002. 'La reprise sceptique du cogito cartésien et la *self-reliance* chez Emerson' in *Revue Française d'Etudes Américaines.* 91: 97-109.

Eakin, John Paul, (ed.) 1991. *American Autobiography: Retrospect and Prospect.* Madison: The University of Wisconsin Press.

--. 1985. *Fictions in Autobiography: Studies in the Art of Self-Invention.* Princeton: Princeton University Press.

Ehrenberg, Alain. 1995. *L'individu incertain.* Paris: Calmann-Lévy.

Elam, Keir. 1980. *The Semiotics of Theatre and Drama.* London: Routledge.

Elias, Norbert. 1987; rpt. 1991. *La société des individus.* Paris: Fayard.

Emerson, Ralph W. 1841. 'Self-reliance' in *Essays: First Series.* Project Gutenberg. http://www.ibiblio.org/gutenberg/etext01/1srwe10.txt. (Accessed December 2002).

--. 1849. 'The American Scholar'. In *Nature: Addresses and Lectures.* http://www.emersoncentral.com/amscholar.htm. (Accessed December 2002).

Charles Ess and the Association of Internet Researchers. 2002. *Ethical Decision-Making and Internet Research: Recommendations*

from the a(o)ir Ethics Working Committeee.
http://www.aoir.org/reports/DraftFIVE.html. (Accessed June
2003).

Evans, Mary. 1997. *Introducing Contemporary Feminist Thought.*
Cambridge: Polity Press.

Evrard, Franck. 1996. *L'humour.* Paris: Hachette.

Field, Susan L. 1997. *The Romance of Desire: Emerson's
Commitment to Incompletion*, Cranbury, NJ: Associated
University Press.

Fisher, Jeffrey. 1996. 'Feminist Cybermaterialism: Gender and the
Body in Cyberspace'. Paper delivered at *Virtue and Virtuality
Conference.* (MIT, 20-21 April 1996).
http://web.mit.edu/womens-studies/www/fisher.html.
(Accessed April 2002).

Flahault, François. 1999. 'Une manière d'être à plusieurs' in Gérald
Cahen (ed.) *La conversation.* Paris: Editions Autrement: 58-
81.

Foot, Kirsten, Schneider, Steve. 2002. 'Online Action: In the US
2000 Political Campaign' *in* Serfaty, Viviane (ed.) *L'Internet
en politique, des Etats-Unis à l'Europe.* Strasbourg: Presses
Universitaires de Strasbourg.

Forster, E. M. 1927, rpt 1963. *Aspects of the Novel.* Harmondsworth:
Penguin.

Foucault, Michel. 1975. *Surveiller et punir: naissance de la prison.*
Paris: Gallimard.

--. *Naissance de la clinique.* 1963; rpt. 1993. Paris: Quadrige/PUF.

Franklin, Benjamin. 1903. *Autobiography*, New-York, T.Y. Crowell.
http://www.ushistory.org/franklin/autobiography/index.htm.
(Accessed December 2003).

Freud, Sigmund. 1905; rpt. 1978. *Jokes and their Relation to the
Unconscious.* London: Hogarth.

--. 1928; rpt. 1978. 'Humour' in Freud, Sigmund, *The Standard
Edition of the Complete Psychological Works.* vol. 21.
London: Hogarth.

Friedman, Susan Stanford. 2000. 'Locational Feminism: Gender,
Cultural Geographies, and Geopolitical Literacy'. Paper
delivered at the IV European Feminist Research Conference
*Body, Gender, Subjectivity: Crossing Borders of Disciplines
and Institutions*, Bologna (Italy), Sept. 28th –Oct. 1st, 2000,
http://www.women.it/cyberarchive/files/stanford.htm.
(Accessed March 2002).

--. 1988. 'Women's Autobiographical Selves: Theory and Practice' *in* Benstock, Shari (ed.) *The Private Self: Theory and Practice of Women's Autobiographical Writings*. Chapel Hill, N.C.: The University of North Carolina Press: 34-62.

Gascoigne, David. 1997. *Le moi et ses espaces: quelques repères identitaires dans la littérature française contemporaine.* Caen: Presses Universitaires de Caen.

Genette, Gérard. 1987. *Seuils.* Paris: Seuil.

Gibson, William. 1984. *Neuromancer*. London: Grafton Books.

Gilman, William *et al.*, (eds). 1960-1982. *The Journals and Miscellaneous Notebooks of Ralph Waldo Emerson.* 16 vols. Cambridge, Massachussetts: Harvard University Press.

Glaser, Mark. 2003. 'The Infectious Desire To be Linked in the Blogosphere'. *Nieman Reports* 57 (3) 87. http://www.nieman.harvard.edu/reports/03-3NRfall/V57N3.pdf. (Accessed October 2003).

Gueissaz, Mireille. 1995. 'Comment devenait-on un 'saint' puritain en Grande-Bretagne au XVIIè siècle ?' *Le for intérieur*. Paris: PUF: 80-96.

Guillaumin, Jean. 1973. 'Freud entre les deux topiques: le comique après "L'humour" (1928), une analyse inachevée'. *Revue française de psychanalyse* 4: 637.

Gusdorf, Gustave. 1956. 'Conditions et limites de l'autobiographie' in *Formen der Selbstdarstellung: Festgabe für Fritz Neubert,* Berlin: Duncker & Humblot: 106-123.

--. 1975. 'De l'autobiographie initiatique à l'autobiographie genre littéraire' in *Revue d'histoire littéraire de la France*, 75: 957-1002.

--. 1991a. *Lignes de vie 1: les écritures du moi*. Paris: Odile Jacob.

--. 1991b. *Lignes de vie 2: auto-bio-graphie*. Paris: Odile Jacob.

Harel, Simon. 1997. *Le récit de soi*. Montréal: XYZ Editeur.

Haroche, Claudine. 1995. 'Le for intérieur: être à soi, se soustraire au pouvoir absolutiste. La philosophie morale et politique de Pierre Charron' in *Le for intérieur*. Paris: PUF: 67-79.

Horkheimer, Max, Adorno, Theodor W. 1944, rpt 1974. 'La production industrielle de biens culturels' in *La dialectique de la raison: fragments philosophiques*. Paris: Gallimard.

Iser, Wolfgang. 1976. *L'acte de lecture: théorie de l'effet esthétique,* (transl. E. Sznycer). Bruxelles: Pierre Mardaga.

Jackson, John E. 1990. 'Mythes du sujet: à propos de

l'autobiographie et de la cure analytique' in *L'autobiographie: VIès rencontres psychanalytiques d'Aix en Provence 1987.* Paris: Les Belles Lettres: 135-169.

Jones, Steve. 1999. *Doing Internet Research: Critical Issues and Methods for Examining the Net.* Thousand Oaks: Sage.

Kagle, Steven E., Gramegna, Lorenza. 1996. 'Rewriting her Life: Fictionalization and the Use of Fictional models in Early American Women's Diaries' in Bunkers, Suzanne L., Huff, Cynthia A. (eds) *Inscribing the Daily: Critical Essays on Women's Diaries.* Amherst: University of Massachussetts Press: 38-55.

Keller, Julia. 1999. 'She has seen the future and it is– Weblogs' in *Chicago Tribune* (Sept.7, 1999) http://pqasb.pqarchiver.com/chicagotribune

Kofman, Sarah. 1985. *La mélancolie de l'art.* Paris: Editions Galilée.

--. 1976. *Autobiogriffures.* Paris: Christian Bourgois.

Kristeva, Julia. 1969. *Sémiotiké: Recherches pour une sémanalyse.* Paris: Seuil.

Kuperty-Tsur, Nadine (ed.). 2000. *Ecriture de soi et argumentation: rhétorique et modèles de l'autoreprésentation. Actes du colloque de l'Université de Tel-Aviv, 3-5 mai 1998.* Caen: Presses Universitaires de Caen.

Lacan, Jacques. 1966. *Ecrits.* Paris: Seuil.

--. 1973a. 'L'Étourdit'. *Scilicet* 4: 5-51.

--. 1973b. 'Les non-dupes errent'. Oral seminar. (November 13, 1973) http://perso.wanadoo.fr/espace.freud/topos/psycha/psysem/no ndup/nondup1.htm. (Accessed September 2003).

Laporte, Roger. 1973. *Fugue: Supplément, biographie.* Paris: Gallimard.

Laugier, Sandra. 2002. ' Emerson: Penser l'ordinaire'. In *Revue Française d'Etudes Américaines.* 91: 43-59.

Le Breton, David. 1999. *L'Adieu au corps.* Paris: Métailié.

Lejeune, Philippe. 1975. *Le pacte autobiographique.* Paris: Seuil.

--. 1993. *Le moi des demoiselles: Enquête sur le journal de jeune fille.* Paris: Seuil.

--. 1998. *Pour l'autobiographie: chroniques.* Paris: Seuil.

--. 2000a. 'Comment finissent les journaux' in Lejeune Philippe, Viollet, Catherine, (eds). *Genèses du 'je': manuscrits et autobiographie.* Paris: CNRS Editions: 209-238.

--. 2000b. *'Cher écran': journal personnel, ordinateur, Internet.* Paris, Seuil.

Lévy, Pierre. 1994. *L'intelligence collective: pour une anthropologie du cyberespace*. Paris: La Découverte.

Levy, Stephen. 2002. 'Living in the Blogosphere'. *Newsweek*. (Aug.26, 2002).

Mabillot, Vincent. 'Du regard à la caresse'. Paper delivered at the *Réseau et Médiation Culturelle Colloquium*.(Université Paris XIII. 30 janvier 2002). http://archivesic.ccsd.cnrs.fr. (Accessed September 2003).

Marin, Louis. 1999. *L'écriture de soi*. Paris: PUF.

Marvin, L.E. 1995. 'Spoof, spam, lurk and lag: The aesthetics of text-based virtual realities' in *Journal of Computer-Mediated Communication*. 1 (2). http://www.usc.edu/dept/annenberg/vol1/issue2/marvin.html

Mattsson, Kristin. 2000. 'Texts of Identities: Life Stories of Swedish-Speaking Women in Finland'. Paper delivered at the IV European Feminist Research Conference *Body, Gender, Subjectivity: Crossing Borders of Disciplines and Institutions*, (Bologna, Italy. Sept. 28th –Oct. 1st, 2000). http://www.women.it/4thfemconf/. (Accessed July 2002).

Mauger, Gérard. 1999. 'Pour une sociologie de la sociologie: notes pour une recherche' in *L'homme et la société*. 131: 101-120.

Médam, Alain. 1983. 'Réflexions de l'objet' in *Actes et recherches sociales: langages et médiations*. 10 (1) 65-78.

Mellon, Thomas. 1984. *A Book of One's Own: People and their Diaries*. New-York: Ticknor and Fields.

Mijolla-Mellor, Sophie de. 1990. 'Survivre à son passé' in *L'autobiographie: VIès rencontres psychanalytiques d'Aix en Provence 1987*. Paris: Les Belles Lettres: 101-128.

Miller, Hugh. 1995. 'The Presentation of Self in Electronic Life: Goffman on the Internet'. Paper presented at *Embodied Knowledge and Virtual Space Conference*, University of London. http://ess.ntu.ac.uk/miller/cyberpsych/goffman.htm. (Accessed September 2003).

Mohanraj, Mary Anne, Hartman, Jed. 2003. "Journals and Community" in *Strange Horizons* (March 31, 2003) http://www.strangehorizons.com/index.pl?contents=/2003/200 30922/editorial.shtml. (Accessed September 2003).

Napolitano, Todd E. 1996. 'Of Graphomania, Confession, and the Writing Self, or The Kitsch of On-Line Journals' in *The*

Electronic Book Review, EBR3.
http://www.altx.com/ebr/reviews/rev3/todd.htm .
(Accessed September 2001)

Neyraut, Michel. 1990. 'De l'autobiographie' in *L'autobiographie: Viès rencontres psychanalytiques d'Aix en Provence 1987.* Paris: Les Belles Lettres: 7-47.

Olney, James. 1981. *Metaphors of Self: The Meaning of Autobiography.* Princeton, N.J.: Princeton University Press.

Ong, Walter J. 1982. *Orality and Literacy: The Technologizing of the Word.* London: Methuen.

Paccagnella, Luciano. 1997. 'Getting the Seat of your Pants Dirty: Strategies for Ethnographic Research on Virtual Communities' in *Journal of Computer-Mediated Communication* 3(1). (Accessed August 1998). http://jcmc.huji.ac.il/vol3/issue1/paccagnella.html#s2.4

Pachet, Pierre. 2001. *Les baromètres de l'âme: naissance du journal intime.* Paris: Hachette.

Passerini , Luisa. 1989. 'Women's Personal Narratives: Myths, Experiences, Emotions' in Barber, Joy W., Farrell, Amy, Garner, Shirley N. *et al.* (eds). *Interpreting Women's Lives: Feminist Theory and Personal Narratives.* Bloomington: Indiana University Press: 189-197.

--. 2000. 'Becoming a Subject in the Time of the Death of the Subject'. Paper delivered at the IV European Feminist Research Conference *Body, Gender, Subjectivity: Crossing Borders of Disciplines and Institutions* (Bologna, Sept. 28th – Oct. 1st, 2000). http://www.women.it/4thfemconf/

Petitat, André. 2001. 'Tyrannie de la transparence et transformations des frontières privé-public' in *Revue des Sciences Sociales de l'Université Marc Bloch.* 28: 40-47.

Pini, Maria. 2000. 'Girls on Film: Video-Diaries as Auto-Ethnographies'. Paper presented at *Body, Gender, Subjectivity: Fourth European Feminist Research Conference.* (Bologna, Italy, Sept. 28-Oct. 1, 2000). http://www.women.it/4thfemconf/ (Accessed September 2001).

Porte, Joel. 1988. 'Emerson: Experiments in Creation' *in* Ford, Boris, (ed.) *American Literature.* London: Penguin Books.

--, Morris, Saundra, (eds). 2001. *Emerson's Prose and Poetry,* New-York: Norton.

Ragland-Sullivan, Ellie, Bracher, Mark (eds). 1991. *Lacan and the*

Subject of Language, New-York: Routledge.

Rey-Flaud, Henri. 2002. *Le démenti pervers: le refoulé et l'oublié*, Paris: Aubier.

Rosé, Daniel. 1989. 'Essai d'évaluation du travail du séminaire' in Shentoub, S.A. ed. *L'humour dans l'œuvre de Freud*. Paris: Two Cities: 18-40.

Rosenberg, Scott. 1999. 'Fear of Links' in *Salon* (May 28) http://www.salon.com/tech/col/rose/1999/05/28/weblo gs/index.html. (Accessed October 2003).

Rosen, Jay. 2003. 'Ten Things Conservative About the Weblog Form in Journalism' in *Press Think* (Oct 17) http://journalism.nyu.edu/pubzone/weblogs/pressthink/2003/1 0/17/conserv_ten.html. (Accessed October 2003).

Rosenwald, Lawrence. 1988. *Emerson and the Art of the Diary*. New-York: Oxford University Press.

Rousseau, Jean-Jacques. 1788; rpt. 1964. *Les confessions*. Paris: Garnier.

Scharf, Barbara F. 1999. 'Beyond Netiquette: The Ethics of Doing Naturalistic Discourse Research on the Internet' in Steve Jones, (ed.) *Doing Internet research: Critical Issues and Methods for Examining the Net*. Thousand Oaks, CA: Sage: 243-256.

Schopenhauer, Arthur. 1969. *The World as Will and Representation*. vol. II. (tr. E. F. J. Payne) New York: Dover.

Serfaty, Viviane. 1999. *L'Internet, l'imaginaire, le politique: perspective comparatiste sur quelques aspects du réseau en France, en Grande-Bretagne, aux Etats-Unis. 2 vols.* PhD dissertation. Université de Paris 7.

--. 2000. 'De la répulsion à la fascination: l'Internet et les représentations des NTIC', *Asp*. 27-30: 231-241.

--. 2002a. 'Showdown on the Internet: Al Gore's and George Bush's Campaign 2000 Websites'. *in* Viviane Serfaty (ed.) *L'Internet en politique, des Etats-Unis à l'Europe*. Strasbourg: Presses Universitaires de Strasbourg.

--. 2002b. 'Forms and Functions of Conflict in Online Communities' in *Cercles* 5 (Spring): 183-197.
http://www.cercles.com/n5/serfaty.pdf

Sibony, Daniel. 1994. 'Bribes de rire et d'humour' in Szafran, A. W., Nysenholc A. (eds) *Freud et le rire*. Paris: Métailié: 71-77.

--. 1995. Le corps et sa danse. Paris: Seuil.

Simonet-Tenant, Françoise. 2001. *Le journal intime*. Paris: Nathan.

Smith, J.C., Ferstman, Carla J. 1990. *The Castration of Oedipus: Feminism, Psychoanalysis and the Will to Power*. New-York: New-York University Press.

Spengemann, William C. 1980. *The Forms of Autobiography: Episodes in the History of a Literary Genre*. New-Haven: Yale University Press.

Starobinski, Jean. 1971. *Jean-Jacques Rousseau: la transparence et l'obstacle*. Paris: Gallimard.

Szafran A. W., Nysenholc A. 1994. 'L'originalité de Freud' in Szafran, A.W., Nysenholc A. (eds) *Freud et le rire*. Paris: Métailié: 11-28.

Tisseron, Serge. 2001. *L'intimité surexposée*. Paris: Ramsay.

Tocqueville, Alexis de. 1840; rpt. 1961. *De la démocratie en Amérique*. Paris: Gallimard.

Turner, Frederick J. 1921. 'The Significance of the Frontier in American History' in *The Frontier in American History*. New-York: Henry Holt &Cy: 1-16.

Wang, Andy. 1999. "Online Digests Help Readers Cope With Avalanche". *New-York Times* (Aug. 2,). http://www.nytimes.com/library/tech/99/08/biztech/articles/02link.html.

Wauthion, Michel, Simon, A.C. (eds). 2000. *Politesse et idéologie: rencontres de pragmatique et de rhétorique conversationnelles*, Louvain-La-Neuve: Peeters.

Weisbuch, Robert. 1999. « Post-Colonial Emerson and the Erasure of Europe », in Joel Porte and Saundra Morris (eds), *The Cambridge Companion to Ralph Waldo Emerson*. Cambridge: Cambridge University Press: 192-217.

Oscar Wilde. 1930. *The Importance of Being Earnest*. London: Everyman's Library.

Winer, Dave. 2002. "The History of Weblogs", *Weblogs.com*. http://newhome.weblogs.com/historyOfWeblogs. (Accessed June 2002).

Wolff, Etienne, ed. 1991. *Cardan: ma vie* (tr. J. Dayre). Paris: Belin.

2. Diaries cited

Al Schroeder's *Novanotes*
  http://www.novanotes.com/feb2002/feb132002.htm
Aiyah's Net
  http://www.aiyah.net/
Augustine's Blog - Blaugustine
  http://www.nataliedarbeloff.com/blaugustine.html
Bev Sykes' *Funny the World*
  http://www.funnytheworld.com/
Beth's *Bad Hair Days*
  http://www.xeney.com/about.html
Bunt Sign
  http://www.buntsign.com/index.html
Bitter Hag
  http://www.bitterhag.com/index.asp
Breakup Babe
  http://breakupbabe.blogspot.com/
Brian's *Blog in A-flat minor*
  http://www.frondle.net/blog/
Carolyn Burke's diary
  http://carolyn.org
Charlie's Daily Web
  http://www.geocities.com/SunsetStrip/9652/report.html
Columbine's *Eccentric Flower*
  http://www.eccentricflower.com/pihua/
Columbine's autobiographyhttp://www.inu.org/pihua/bio.htm
Confessions of an ADD Physics Major
  http://youngaddfemale.blogspot.com
Daze Reader
  http://www.dazereader.com/weblog.htm
Debra Hydes's *Pursed Lips*
  http://www.pursedlips.com
DeeGee Girl Diary
  http://deegeegirl.blogspot.com/
Diane Patterson's *Nobody Knows Anything*
  http://www.nobody-knows-anything.com
Dirty Feet and Lily-White Intentions
  http://lilywhiteintentions.com
Doug Franklin's Journal

http://nilknarf.net
Gingko's *Dreaming Among the Jade Clouds*
http://www.jade-leaves.com/journal/
Greg Van Eekhout's *The Official Voice of the American People*
http://www.journalscape.com/greg/
Her Desires
http://www.herdesires.net
Houston's blog
http://h-townblogs.blogspot.com/
Jessamyn's *Internet Persona*
http://jessamyn.diary-x.com/?entry=default
Kevin's *Change Over Time*
http://kevin.diary-x.com/
Ladybug's blog
http://ladybug.notsweet.net/
Lisa's Journey
http://www.section12.com/users/lisa_p/
Mary Anne's *Ongoing, Erratic Journal*
http://www.mamohanraj.com/Diary/diary.html
Medea Sin
http://www.medeasin.com/jindex.htm
Meditations of a Sweet Jezebel
http://wickedjezebel.blogspot.com/
The Mighty Kymm's *Sweet as a Biscuit*
http://www.sweetasabiscuit.com/mightykymm/
Miles Hochstein's *Documented Life*
http://www.documentedlife.com/welcome.htm
Miriam H. Nadel's *Areas of Unrest*
http://www.areasofunrest.net
Naked Loft Party
http://www.nakedloftparty.blogspot.com/
Rachel's Daily Diary
http://www.reinyday.com/rachel/daily
Reality Asylum Voice Project – Phase 2
http://www.xs4all.nl/~rienz/asylum/vp2.html
Sam Snyder's *Continuum*
http://www.itwarren.com/continuum/weblog/weblog000013.s
html
Shmuel's *Soapbox*
http://www.babeltower.org/soapbox

Subsequent Events
   http://www.amyd.org/about.html .
Terri's *Footnotes*
   http://www.secraterri.com
Tomato Nation
   http://www.tomatonation.com

3. Archives and webrings

The Internet Archive
   http://mail.archive.org/index.html
Glass Houses
   http://www.cmp.ucr.edu/students/glasshouses
The Online Diary History Project
   http://www.diaryhistoryproject.com.
Open Pages
   http://hedgehog.net
Diary Land
   http://www.diaryland.com/
Diarist Net
   http://www.diarist.net
The Live Webcam Ring
   http://m.webring.com/hub?ring=livecams
Diary-X
   http://www.diary-x.com/
The Rice Bowl Journals
   http://ricebowljournals.com
Section 12
   http://section12.com

4. Political blogs cited

William Quick, *Daily Pundit*
   http://www.iw3p.com/DailyPundit
Glenn Reynolds' *Instapundit*
   http://www.instapundit.com

5. Miscellaneous

BoingBoing
    http://boingboing.net
Perseus White Papers
    http://www.perseus.com/blogsurvey
Rebecca's Pocket
    http://www.rebeccablood.net/

Index